# Information Theory

Saving Bits

CONTEMPORARY APPLIED MATHEMATICS

# Information Theory

## Saving Bits

**William Sacco**
**Wayne Copes**
**Clifford Sloyer**
**Robert Stark**

JANSON PUBLICATIONS, INC.   Providence, Rhode Island

Material based on work supported by the National Science Foundation.

# Contents

The authors wish to thank John Jameson, Jane Melville, A. Brinton Cooper, III, and Richard Crouse, who helped to produce this monograph.

# Introduction

In the bestseller *Megatrends*, John Naisbitt describes America's shift from an industrial society to an information society. He reports that 1956 was the first year that more Americans worked with information than produced goods. In the next year the information revolution began spreading to all the world. The Soviets launched Sputnik, which not only began the space age, but more importantly introduced the era of global satellite communications. Today's space shuttle can orbit a 65,000 pound payload, 355 times the weight of Sputnik, and much more sophisticated. Global communications are commonplace.

There is an increasing demand for efficient data storage and transmission in large-scale, high-speed data networks for the exchange of information in the military, government, and industry. One large network exists just to support the two Voyager spacecraft that were launched from Earth in 1977 bound for the giant planets in the solar system, Jupiter, Saturn, and Uranus, the last of which was visited in January 1986.

The Voyagers have five cameras that take a wide variety of pictures (visible light, infra-red, ultra-violet), and six other instruments for measuring the presence of elements or compounds on a planet or in a planetary atmosphere. The Voyagers have transmitted 4 trillion bits (0's or 1's) of scientific data since they were launched. (Four trillion bits is enough to represent 5,000 sets of the *Encyclopaedia Britannica*.)

In most communication systems, information is coded into strings of bits. For example, the Voyagers may code and transmit a black and white photograph of Jupiter by a million strings. Each string represents a gray level (shades of gray from white to black), corresponding to the intensity of light reflected from a small region of the scene.

When a Voyager spacecraft is behind a planet it cannot immediately send data to Earth. At such times an on-board, digital tape recorder stores the data for later playback to Earth. As can be imagined, the experimenters often would like to record more data than the tape recorder can hold. The communications engineer is challenged to find more efficient ways to store data. Among other things, you will learn about efficient storage techniques in this monograph.

In the two-way communication with the Voyager spacecraft, the uplink is for the command data going from the command center (on Earth) to the spacecraft, and the downlink is used to return the scientific and engineering data to Earth. Engineering data come from monitors that determine the attitude and position of the spacecraft and the status of on-board instruments and subsystems, while scientific data come from observational instruments of various types.

The command and engineering data are sent at slow rates because errors in transmission can lead to wrong commands with disastrous effects such as losing contact with the spacecraft. Stringent requirements are imposed to insure the accurate transmission of these data. Sophisticated techniques are used to keep the errors in the decoded string to fewer than one bit per billion.

The scientific data are sent at faster rates (of 4.8 to 21.6 thousand bits per second), and are required to have fewer than one error in 100,000 bits after decoding. Hence, these data are also coded so that transmission errors can be corrected. In the process, redundant bits (extra bits) are added to the data in such a way that bits lost, from radio frequency interference or rain or whatever, can be reconstructed. In the early years of the Voyager missions, Golay coding added one redundant bit for every information bit sent to Earth. More recently, Voyager has been reprogrammed to use the very efficient Reed-Solomon code, which adds one redundant bit for every three bits of raw scientific data sent to Earth.

The communications network for the NASA (National Aeronautics and Space Administration) Space Telescope Program will have to be even more sophisticated than the Voyager network. The Space Telescope will be photographing and sensing the heavens while orbiting at 320 miles above the Earth. The photographs (and engineering data) will be sent in the form of binary strings to a NASA center in New Mexico by way of a satellite orbiting 22,000 miles above the Earth. Commands from Earth will also be relayed to the Space Telescope by way of another satellite orbiting 22,000 miles above the Earth.

To get these messages through with acceptable error rates, communication engineers employ a collection of ingenious techniques with such interesting names as K-redundant codes, (20, 12) Golay codes, Hamming codes, Reed–Solomon coding, and Interleaving. As with the Voyager missions, some of the accuracies required are phenomenal. For example, one of the objectives of the mission is to search for pulsars. It has been estimated that some pulsars might remain undetected if the high-speed photometer data is transmitted with any bit error rate greater than one in 100,000. In this monograph you will learn a great deal about error-control methods.

## The Compact Disc

Imagine a concert of your favorite music, played by performers of your own choosing, right in your own home. They eat a lot, smoke a lot, tune up a lot, tie up the phones and the bathrooms, and may not want to leave when the party is over. But just imagine, there'd be no record scratches to interfere with your enjoyment of the music.

Since the early 1980s, stereo buffs and music lovers alike have been enjoying the next best thing—music recorded on compact discs, CDs, using digital audio technology. Even before the CDs and their players became available, many ordinary LP records and cassette tapes were being made from "digital master" tapes. The improvement in sound quality with digital mastering is noticeable and pleasant, but the changes brought by CDs are remarkable. While there are debates among purists over the finer points, it is generally agreed that CDs reproduce music more faithfully than earlier techniques. The low sounds are more prominent, the high sounds are clearer and more brilliant. Individual instruments and voices are more easily heard against the ensemble. Finally, the noise, distortion, hiss, pops, crackles, and all the other annoying and unwanted sounds in the music are *gone!*

How is this done? What sorts of breakthroughs in science and engineering have made such improvements possible? The ability to do more and more things with smaller and smaller electronic "chips" has made it possible to put into practice the same error-correction techniques that are used in billion-dollar space communication networks. Application of these techniques to create the noise-free compact disc system will be described in Part II of the monograph.

## Part I

# EFFICIENT STORAGE AND TRANSMISSION OF INFORMATION IN THE ABSENCE OF NOISE

## A.  Saving Time and Space

In information transmission, the emphasis is on sending needed information quickly.  What's needed will vary with the application.  In a particular scientific application, it may be sufficient to send only estimates of measurements from infra-red sensors scanning regions of the sky.  For example, it may be enough to transmit only the interval $R_i$ which contains measurement $R$:

| $R_1$ | $R_2$ | $R_3$ | $R_4$ |
|-------|-------|-------|-------|
| $R < b$ | $b \leq R < c$ | $c \leq R < d$ | $d \leq R$ |

If so, we could code the 4 intervals as follows:

| Interval | $R_1$ | $R_2$ | $R_3$ | $R_4$ |
|----------|-------|-------|-------|-------|
| Code | 00 | 01 | 10 | 11 |

The 0's and 1's are called bits (short for binary digits) and the code is called a binary code because it uses only 0's and 1's.  The code for each interval is called a code word.  The 0's and 1's can be represented and sent as pulses.  For example, the 1 can be sent as a millisecond (1/1000 of a second) pulse of amplitude $X$.  A zero may be sent as a millisecond pulse of much larger amplitude, say $4X$.

A message of estimated measurements

$$R_2 \, R_1 \, R_3 \, R_1 \, R_4 \, R_1 \, R_2 \, R_1$$

would be coded as a string of bits:

$$0100100011000100.$$

1.  How many bits are required per measurement?  _____

Since each measurement requires 2 bits, the average number of bits per code word is 2 also, and the cost per code word is 2 bits.

2.  Decode the messages:

    a.  01100100 _____

    b.  0000000000000000 _____

    c.  10010110000010001000 _____

    d.  00001111010101101010 _____

Can you do better than 2 bits per measurement?
You might be tempted to use the seemingly more efficient code:

$$R_1 \quad R_2 \quad R_3 \quad R_4$$
$$0 \quad \ 1 \quad \ 00 \quad \ 11$$

The message $R_1 R_3 R_2 R_4$ would be coded as 000111.

**3a.** Using this new code, decode the string 010000111. _____

You probably concluded that this code produces strings that can be decoded in several different ways. In fact, it could be interpreted as

$$R_1 \ R_2 \ R_1 \ R_1 \ R_1 \ R_1 \ R_2 \ R_2 \ R_2$$

or

$$R_1 \ R_2 \ R_1 \ R_1 \ R_3 \ R_2 \ R_4$$

or

$$R_1 \ R_2 \ R_3 \ R_3 \ R_4 \ R_1$$

or

nine other ways.

**3b.** Find 2 other interpretations of 010000111.

---

Such a code is not useful. To be useful, the decoding rules must give only one interpretation for any string of bits: that is, the code must be *uniquely decodable*. A code is uniquely decodable if all messages sent can be reconstructed perfectly from the coded binary strings. In a constant-length code, like the first one considered, each codeword has the same number of bits. In that case, each codeword had two bits. With a defined codeword length, and a key (table of interpretations for all possible codewords), unique decodability is assured.

If the codewords are not all the same length, the decoding rules must provide the decoder some other means of telling where a codeword ends. The prefix property is one such means. A code has the *prefix property* if no codeword is a prefix of (first part of) another codeword. If a code has the prefix property, it is uniquely decodable.

The code   00  01  10  11   has the prefix property.

So does the code   0  10  110  111.

Constant-length codes generally have the prefix property; but the property must be designed into codes of variable length. The code   0  1  00  11 does not have the prefix property since 0 is a prefix (the first symbol of 00) and 1 is a prefix of 11.

Economies of the code   00  01  10  11   may be possible if you take into account the *frequencies* with which the intervals $R_1$, $R_2$, $R_3$, $R_4$ occur. By "economies," we mean reductions in the average number of bits per measurement.

Suppose the 4 infra-red intervals occur, on the average, with the proportions:

| Interval | $R_1$ | $R_2$ | $R_3$ | $R_4$ |
|----------|-------|-------|-------|-------|
| Proportion | 1/2 | 1/4 | 1/8 | 1/8 |

Try the code

| $R_1$ | $R_2$ | $R_3$ | $R_4$ |
|-------|-------|-------|-------|
| 0 | 10 | 110 | 111 |

**4.** Does the code have the prefix property? _____

The message $R_2 R_1 R_3 R_1 R_4 R_1 R_2 R_1$ is coded as 10011001110100.

**5.** Code the messages
  a.  $R_2 R_2 R_1 R_1 R_1 R_3 R_3$ _____
  b.  $R_1 R_1 R_2 R_1 R_3 R_4$ _____

**6.** Decode the messages
  a.  10100000011011111000010 _____
  b.  0010110111000010110 _____

What is the average cost in bits per measurement of the code   0   10   110   111   with the proportions   1/2   1/4   1/8   1/8?

On the average, over the long run,

for 1/2 of the occasions, $R_1$ occurs and it has a 1 bit code word;

for 1/4 of the occasions, $R_2$ occurs and it has a 2 bit code word;

for 1/8 of the occasions, $R_3$ occurs and it has a 3 bit code word;

for 1/8 of the occasions, $R_4$ occurs and it has a 3 bit code word.

Hence, on the average, the cost is $\frac{1}{2}(1) + \frac{1}{4}(2) + \frac{1}{8}(3) + \frac{1}{8}(3)$ or $1\frac{3}{4}$ bits per measurement.

This is a 12.5% decrease[1] from the cost of the code   00   01   10   11   which was 2 bits per measurement. The accumulated savings of many such improvements make more ambitious projects possible.

**7.** Try to find a code which is uniquely decodable and more economical than $1\frac{3}{4}$ bits/measurement for the case:

| Interval | $R_1$ | $R_2$ | $R_3$ | $R_4$ |
|----------|-------|-------|-------|-------|
| Proportion of occurrence | 1/2 | 1/4 | 1/8 | 1/8 |

---

[1]The 12.5% decrease is determined as follows:

$$\frac{2 - 1\frac{3}{4}}{2} = \frac{\frac{1}{4}}{2} = \frac{1}{8} = 12.5\%.$$

# B. Shannon's Theorem

We are certain that you did not find a better code. A theorem by Claude Shannon, the famous "Father of Information Theory," guarantees that 1.75 bits/measurement is the smallest cost possible for the proportions 1/2, 1/4, 1/8, 1/8.

To explain the theorem, we need a bit of terminology.

A set of *elements* such as the infra-red measurement intervals $R_1$, $R_2$, $R_3$, $R_4$ or the letters of the English alphabet, is called a *source*. The average proportions of occurrence of the elements are called the *probabilities of the source*. For the infra-red intervals the source probabilities were 1/2, 1/4, 1/8, 1/8.

A source is called *independent* if the occurrence of an element does not influence the probability of occurrence of the next element. Ordinary English is not an independent source since an H is much more likely to follow a T than it is to follow an X, and a U is most likely after a Q.

We can now state Shannon's Source Coding Theorem for binary codes:

Given an independent source having *k* elements, with probabilities of occurrence $p_1, \ldots, p_k$, then

1. The cost of the code in bits/element is greater than or equal to

$$-[p_1\log_2 p_1 + \cdots + p_k\log_2 p_k].$$

2. Uniquely decodable codes exist with cost (average code word length) as close to $-[p_1\log_2 p_1 + \cdots + p_k\log_2 p_k]$ as you care to achieve.

The quantity $\log_2(x)$ is the power of 2 that equals *x*. Hence $\log_2(16) = 4$ since $2^4 = 16$ and $\log_2(1/8) = -3$ since $2^{-3} = 1/2^3 = 1/8$.

The highly efficient codes that are promised in the second part of the theorem are attainable by a trick known as block coding, which will shortly be explained.

The quantity $I = -[p_1\log_2 p_1 + \cdots + p_k\log_2 p_k]$ has various names. Two popular names are *entropy* and *average information content*, and so we speak of the entropy or information content of an independent source.

8. Compute

   $\log_2(1/4)$   ————————

   $\log_2(1/2)$   ————————

   $\log_2(2)$   ————————

   $\log_2(4)$   ————————

   $\log_2(1/16)$   ————————

   $\log_2(1)$   ————————

   $\log_2(1/256)$   ————————

   $\log_2(1/4096)$   ————————

9. Using Table 1, determine

   $\log_2(6/10)$   ————————

   $\log_2(3/10)$   ————————

$\log_2(1/1000)$  _____

$\log_2(99/100)$  _____

Logs to the base 2 of fractions that are not powers of 2 are given in several communication engineering books for ready accessibility.

## Table 1

### Logarithms to the base 2
### for selected probability values ($P$)

| $P$ | $-\text{LOG}_2 P$ |
|---|---|
| 0.001 | 9.9658 |
| 0.005 | 7.6439 |
| 0.01 | 6.6439 |
| 0.03 | 5.0589 |
| 0.05 | 4.3219 |
| 0.10 | 3.3219 |
| 0.16 | 2.6439 |
| 0.20 | 2.3219 |
| 0.30 | 1.7370 |
| 0.40 | 1.3219 |
| 0.50 | 1.0000 |
| 0.60 | 0.7370 |
| 0.70 | 0.5146 |
| 0.80 | 0.3219 |
| 0.81 | 0.3040 |
| 0.90 | 0.1520 |
| 0.99 | 0.0145 |
| 1.00 | 0.0000 |

10. Compute the entropy for the following source probabilities.

a.
$p_1$  $p_2$
1/2  1/2  _____

b.
$p_1$  $p_2$  $p_3$  $p_4$
1/4  1/4  1/4  1/4  _____

c.
$p_1$  $p_2$  $p_3$  $p_4$
1/2  1/4  1/8  1/8  _____

d.
$p_1$  $p_2$  $p_3$  $p_4$  $p_5$  $p_6$  $p_7$  $p_8$
1/4  1/4  1/8  1/8  1/16  1/16  1/16  1/16

_____

11. Using Table 2, determine the entropy for the following source probabilities.

a.
$p_1$  $p_2$
7/10  3/10  _____

b.
$p_1$  $p_2$
8/10  2/10  _____

By examining the expression for Statement I in Shannon's Theorem, you can see that the entropy is never negative, since the logarithms of probabilities are never positive. A proof of the Shannon Theorem is given in the Shannon reference in the Suggested Readings.

**Table 2**

**Entropies for selected two-element**
$P$, $(1 - P)$ **source probabilities**

| $P$ | $I$ |
|---|---|
| 0 | 0 |
| 0.001 | 0.0114 |
| 0.010 | 0.0808 |
| 0.10 | 0.4690 |
| 0.20 | 0.7219 |
| 0.30 | 0.8813 |
| 0.40 | 0.9710 |
| 0.50 | 1.0000 |
| 0.60 | 0.9710 |
| 0.70 | 0.8813 |
| 0.80 | 0.7219 |
| 0.90 | 0.4690 |
| 0.99 | 0.0808 |
| 0.999 | 0.0114 |
| 1.00 | 0 |

Please return to Exercise 7. You see from Exercise 10c that the entropy is 1.75. Hence if the source in Exercise 7 is independent, the code   0    10   110    111    is the best possible according to the Shannon Theorem.

12. Suppose you require 8 levels $(L_1, \ldots, L_8)$ of infra-red measurements instead of 4 levels. Suppose these levels constitute an independent source with probabilities of occurrence:

| Level | 1 | 2 | 3 | 4 | 5 | 6 | 7 | 8 |
|---|---|---|---|---|---|---|---|---|
| Probabilities | 1/4 | 1/4 | 1/8 | 1/8 | 1/16 | 1/16 | 1/16 | 1/16 |

a. Compute the entropy for this source. (Did you do this computation before?)

Entropy: _____

b. Try to find a code with the prefix property whose average code word length equals the entropy.

| Level | 1 | 2 | 3 | 4 | 5 | 6 | 7 | 8 |
|---|---|---|---|---|---|---|---|---|
| Code | | | | | | | | |

Suppose you are required to transmit an independent source consisting of only the symbols A and B with probabilities $p(A) = 7/10$, $p(B) = 3/10$.

An obvious code is

$$
\begin{array}{cc}
A & B \\
0 & 1
\end{array}
$$

**13.** Does this code have the prefix property? _____
Is it uniquely decodable? _____

**14.** What is the cost (average code word length) for this code? _____

**15.** Is this the most economical code? _____

It certainly seems so!!! Before concluding that   0   1   is the best code, we had better consult the Shannon Theorem.

**16.** Use Table 2 or Exercise 11a to determine the entropy of the source.

_____

(Note that by Shannon's Theorem you should be able to find a code with cost as close to the entropy as you desire.)

The entropy was 0.88. Surprise! Shannon indicates you should be able to find a code with cost as close to 0.88 as you desire.

The code can be improved if pairs of letters are used. (A pair of letters is called a *digram*; letter triplets are called *trigrams*.) $p(XY) = p(X)p(Y)$ for an independent source (for example, $p(A)p(B) = .7 \times .3 = .21$), so the probabilities are as follows:

$$p(AA) = .49, \quad p(AB) = .21, \quad p(BA) = .21, \quad p(BB) = .09.$$

Try the code

$$
\begin{array}{cccc}
AA & AB & BA & BB \\
0 & 10 & 110 & 111
\end{array}
$$

**17.** Find the cost (average code word length) for this code. _____

The answer represents a 10% saving over one bit per letter, and would be considered a big improvement.

**18.** Try to improve the code by trigrams. Note that

$$
\begin{aligned}
p(AAA) &= .343, & p(BBB) &= .027, \\
p(AAB) &= p(ABA) = p(BAA) = .147, \\
p(ABB) &= p(BAB) = p(BBA) = .063.
\end{aligned}
$$

Codes that bunch (combine) source element symbols are called block codes. Digrams and trigrams are examples of block codes. Shannon's theorem allows for block codes to achieve the lowest possible cost. In most real situations, block codes are required to achieve a desired cost.

Morse code is not a binary code because it uses 3 code signals—dot, dash, and between-letter pause—to code the alphabet. Several letters and their International Morse codes follow.

| Letter | | A | E | J | O | T | Z |
|---|---|---|---|---|---|---|---|
| Morse Code | | .— | . | .——— | ——— | — | ——.. |

19. (Optional) Write a computer program for computing entropy. Use your program to compute the entropy of the source probabilities ($p_t$) from Table 3, presuming that the source is independent.

## Table 3

### Binary Codes for English text

| $L_t$ | $p_t$ | Code 1 | Code 2 | Code 3 | $log_2 p_t$ |
|---|---|---|---|---|---|
| | .1859 | 00000 | 00 | 000 | 2.4 |
| A | .0642 | 00001 | 10100 | 0100 | 4.0 |
| B | .0127 | 00010 | 0111100 | 011111 | 6.3 |
| C | .0218 | 00011 | 01101100 | 11111 | 5.5 |
| D | .0317 | 00100 | 011100 | 01011 | 5.0 |
| E | .1031 | 00101 | 100 | 101 | 2.9 |
| F | .0208 | 00110 | 1101100 | 001100 | 5.6 |
| G | .0152 | 00111 | 0101100 | 011101 | 6.0 |
| H | .0467 | 01000 | 111100 | 1110 | 4.4 |
| I | .0575 | 01001 | 1100 | 1000 | 4.1 |
| J | .0008 | 01010 | 101010100 | 0111001110 | 10.4 |
| K | .0049 | 01011 | 0110100 | 01110010 | 7.7 |
| L | .0321 | 01100 | 1011100 | 01010 | 5.0 |
| M | .0198 | 01101 | 010100 | 001101 | 5.7 |
| N | .0574 | 01110 | 01100 | 1001 | 4.1 |
| O | .0632 | 01111 | 01010100 | 0110 | 4.0 |
| P | .0152 | 10000 | 10101100 | 011110 | 6.0 |
| Q | .0008 | 10001 | 010110100 | 0111001101 | 10.4 |
| R | .0484 | 10010 | 101100 | 1101 | 4.4 |
| S | .0514 | 10011 | 11100 | 1100 | 4.3 |
| T | .0796 | 10100 | 0100 | 0010 | 3.7 |
| U | .0228 | 10101 | 110100 | 11110 | 5.5 |
| V | .0083 | 10110 | 1110100 | 0111000 | 6.9 |
| W | .0175 | 10111 | 1010100 | 001110 | 5.8 |
| X | .0013 | 11000 | 01110100 | 0111001100 | 9.6 |
| Y | .0164 | 11001 | 011010100 | 001111 | 5.9 |
| Z | .0005 | 11010 | 01011100 | 0111001111 | 11.0 |

The three codes of Table 3 code English letters with the binary digits 0 and 1. Each code has the prefix property. Code 1 is the binary number equivalent of the row number of the letter as given in the table, minus one (for example, the code for letter B is in the third row and the binary equivalent of 2 is 00010).

Code 2 of Table 3 is International Morse Code with 1, 01, and 00 substituted for dot, dash, and between-letter pause. Code 3 is an example of a *Huffman code*. The letter probabilities in the second column of Table 3 are taken from Dr. E. N. Gilbert's paper cited in the Suggested Readings. The first value .1859 is for the between-word space.

20. What is the average code word length for Code 1? _____

**21.** (Optional) Write a computer program to compute average code word length. Use your program to compute the average code word lengths for codes 2 and 3 of Table 3.

The results of the previous exercise show that the Huffman code is substantially better than the Morse Code. The word length is very near the minimum calculated in Exercise 19.

## C. Huffman Coding for Storage of Information

Huffman coding is becoming increasingly popular for compacting data for computer storage. For a given set of source probabilities, the Huffman process generates a highly efficient variable-length code in which the prefix property is guaranteed. After a few preliminaries, the process will be explained.

Each computer has a set of characters that it can input and output. More sophisticated character sets include control codes, capital and small letters, the 10 digits, many punctuation marks (space, period, comma, colon, ... ), mathematical symbols (+, −, /, <, ...), and sometimes Greek letters, which are used frequently as mathematical symbols.

To transfer these characters into the computer, each one is assigned a number; for example, A = 65, H = 72, < = 60, and so on. Present-day computers use either a 6-, 7-, 8-, or 9-bit code to represent the numbers. A six-bit code allows for $2^6 = 64$ characters; a seven-bit code, 128 characters.

**22.** How many characters can be represented by

an 8-bit code? _____ a 9-bit code? _____

To develop a Huffman code for 128 characters, or even a smaller set of only 64 characters, is quite a tedious task, if the work is done by hand. To illustrate the method, we will build a Huffman code to solve Exercise 18, which involves just eight characters, namely the trigrams

AAA  AAB  ABA  ABB  BAA  BAB  BBA  BBB

In Exercise 18 we are given $p(A) =.7$, $p(B) =.3$. The probability of ABA, for example, is therefore

$$p(ABA) = p(A)p(B)p(A) =.7 \times .3 \times .7 =.147.$$

The first step is to find the eight probabilities and arrange the trigrams in ascending order of their probabilities, as shown below:

(1)  BBB  BBA  BAB  ABB  BAA  ABA  AAB  AAA
     .027  .063  .063  .063  .147  .147  .147  .343

Next, add the two smallest probabilities together, underline them, and join them by arrows to their sum. A bar is placed over the sum to provide a terminus for the arrows.

(2)  BBB  BBA  BAB  ABB  BAA  ABA  AAB  AAA
     .027  .063  .063  .063  .147  .147  .147  .343

.090

Next, add the two smallest remaining values, and underline them:

(3)  BBB  BBA  BAB  ABB  BAA  ABA  AAB  AAA
     .027  .063  .063  .063  .147  .147  .147  .343

.090       .126

At this point, the two smallest values that have not been combined yet are .090 and .126. It makes no difference that these are subtotals rather than original probabilities. We add them together and underline to show that they have been combined

(4)  BBB  BBA  BAB  ABB  BAA  ABA  AAB  AAA
     .027  .063  .063  .063  .147  .147  .147  .343

.090       .126

.216

Now, the two smallest lacking underlines (that is, uncombined) are any two of the three original values equalling .147. We choose the rightmost pair for a reason that will soon be clear, and we then have

(5)  BBB  BBA  BAB  ABB  BAA  ABA  AAB  AAA
     .027  .063  .063  .063  .147  .147  .147  .343

.090       .126            .294

.216

Next we obtain

(6)  BBB  BBA  BAB  ABB  BAA  ABA  AAB  AAA
     .027  .063  .063  .063  .147  .147  .147  .343

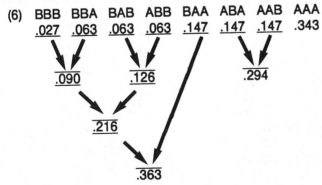

.090       .126            .294

.216

.363

After two more steps we have

(7)
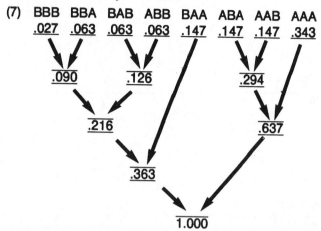

Observe that the completed picture looks like a tree of which the grand total (1.000) is the trunk and the original characters are the uppermost leaves. By choosing the rightmost pair at step 5, we were able to complete the tree without crossing one branch over another. With many more characters, the picture may become a very tangled web.

To read off the code for a character, begin at that character and descend through the tree to the grand total (1.000), noting at each stage whether descent is by the left branch or the right branch of the two branches joining at the next subtotal; doing so, we obtain the following list:

| BBB | BBA | BAB | ABB | BAA | ABA | AAB | AAA |
|-----|-----|-----|-----|-----|-----|-----|-----|
| L | R | L | R | R | L | R | R |
| L | L | R | R | L | L | L | R |
| L | L | L | L | | R | R | |
| L | L | L | L | | | | |

Next, read these codes backwards (from the bottom up), and substitute 1 for L, 0 for R (or the reverse), to obtain the Huffman codes:

| | | |
|-----|------|------|
| BBB | 1111 | .027 |
| BBA | 1110 | .063 |
| BAB | 1101 | .063 |
| ABB | 1100 | .063 |
| BAA | 10   | .147 |
| ABA | 011  | .147 |
| AAB | 010  | .147 |
| AAA | 00   | .343 |

We have entered the probabilities in the rightmost column of this listing for convenience in computing the average bit length of a trigram, which is 2.726, or .909 bits per letter. This is not as good as the digram code which was .905 bits per letter. Nonetheless, Shannon's Theorem guarantees that $n$-grams (as $n$ gets big) will approach .881 bits per letter. So further improvement can be expected with longer blocks. As you saw, however, there may not be an improvement with each step (monograms to digrams to trigrams to 4-grams to 5-grams, etc.).

## Table 4

### ASCII Characters and Illustrative Probabilities

The 7-bit code for each character is the binary number equivalent of the Row Number RN.

Column Headings:  RN = Row Number
                  ON = Octal Number
                  CH = Character
                  PR = Probability

If the RN is followed by an asterisk, an explanatory note will be found at the end of the table.

| RN | ON | CH | PR | RN | ON | CH | PR |
|----|----|----|----|----|----|----|----|
| 0–7* | 0–7 | CT | .0008 | 44* | 54 | , | .0075 |
|  |  |  |  | 45* | 55 | - | .0043 |
| 8* | 10 | BS | .0036 | 46 | 56 | • | .0080 |
|  |  |  |  | 47 | 57 | / | .0010 |
| 9–12 | 11–14 | CT | .0004 |  |  |  |  |
|  |  |  |  | 48 | 60 | 0 | .0012 |
| 13* | 15 | CR | .0140 | 49 | 61 | 1 | .0012 |
|  |  |  |  | 50 | 62 | 2 | .0012 |
| 14–31 | 16–37 | CT | .0018 | 51 | 63 | 3 | .0012 |
| 32* | 40 | SP | .1646 | 52 | 64 | 4 | .0012 |
| 33 | 41 | ! | .0002 | 53 | 65 | 5 | .0011 |
| 34 | 42 | ” | .0014 | 54 | 66 | 6 | .0011 |
| 35 | 43 | # | .0001 | 55 | 67 | 7 | .0011 |
| 36 | 44 | $ | .0001 | 56 | 70 | 8 | .0011 |
| 37 | 45 | % | .0001 | 57 | 71 | 9 | .0011 |
| 38 | 46 | & | .0001 | 58 | 72 | : | .0003 |
| 39* | 47 | ’ | .0011 | 59 | 73 | ; | .0001 |
| 40 | 50 | ( | .0011 | 60 | 74 | < | .0001 |
| 41 | 51 | ) | .0011 | 61 | 75 | = | .0001 |
| 42 | 52 | * | .0001 | 62 | 76 | > | .0001 |
| 43 | 53 | + | .0001 | 63 | 77 | ? | .0003 |
| 64 | 100 | @ | .0001 | 92 | 134 | \ | .0001 |
| 65 | 101 | A | .0016 | 93 | 135 | ] | .0001 |
| 66 | 102 | B | .0003 | 94 | 136 | ˆ | .0001 |
| 67 | 103 | C | .0012 | 95* | 137 | _ | .0036 |
| 68 | 104 | D | .0008 | 96* | 140 | ‘ | .0001 |
| 69 | 105 | E | .0017 | 97 | 141 | a | .0590 |
| 70 | 106 | F | .0008 | 98 | 142 | b | .0117 |
| 71 | 107 | G | .0005 | 99 | 143 | c | .0201 |
| 72 | 110 | H | .0006 | 100 | 144 | d | .0292 |
| 73 | 111 | I | .0018 | 101 | 145 | e | .0945 |
| 74 | 112 | J | .0008 | 102 | 146 | f | .0192 |
| 75 | 113 | K | .0003 | 103 | 147 | g | .0140 |

### Table 4 (cont.)

| RN | ON | CH | PR | RN | ON | CH | PR |
|----|----|----|------|------|----|-----|-------|
| 76 | 114 | L | .0005 | 104 | 150 | h | .0429 |
| 77 | 115 | M | .0007 | 105 | 151 | i | .0529 |
| 78 | 116 | N | .0009 | 106 | 152 | j | .0009 |
| 79 | 117 | O | .0005 | 107 | 153 | k | .0046 |
| 80 | 120 | P | .0008 | 108 | 154 | l | .0295 |
| 81 | 121 | Q | .0001 | 109 | 155 | m | .0182 |
| 82 | 122 | R | .0005 | 110 | 156 | n | .0526 |
| 83 | 123 | S | .0023 | 111 | 157 | o | .0581 |
| 84 | 124 | T | .0034 | 112 | 160 | p | .0140 |
| 85 | 125 | U | .0006 | 113 | 161 | q | .0009 |
| 86 | 126 | V | .0016 | 114 | 162 | r | .0444 |
| 87 | 127 | W | .0008 | 115 | 163 | s | .0472 |
| 88 | 130 | X | .0001 | 116 | 164 | t | .0731 |
| 89 | 131 | Y | .0002 | 117 | 165 | u | .0210 |
| 90 | 132 | Z | .0001 | 118 | 166 | v | .0077 |
| 91 | 133 | [ | .0001 | 119 | 167 | w | .0161 |
| 120 | 170 | x | .0013 | 124* | 174 | \| | .0001 |
| 121 | 171 | y | .0151 | 125 | 175 | } | .0001 |
| 122 | 172 | z | .0005 | 126* | 176 | ~ | .0001 |
| 123 | 173 | { | .0001 | 127* | 177 | DEL | .0001 |

### Explanatory Notes

(A) Characters by Row Number RN:

| RN | Note | RN | Note |
|----|------|----|------|
| 0–7 | CT=Controls | 46 | Period |
| 8 | BS=Back Space | 95 | Underline |
| 13 | CR=Carriage Return | 96 | Backward Apostrophe |
| 32 | SP=Between-Word Space | 124 | Vertical Bar |
| 39 | Apostrophe | 126 | Tilde |
| 44 | Comma | 127 | DEL=Delete |
| 45 | Hyphen (Minus) | | |

(B) The Octal Numbers are included because the 7-bit ASCII codes are most conveniently derived by translating the octal digits into their 3-bit binary equivalents. For example, at RN(83) we find ON(123) and the code for capital S is therefore 001 010 011, or 1010011 without the leading zeros.

(C) The probability values in this table are illustrative only. They are based partly on Table 3, partly on frequencies counted over the Introduction, and partly on fiction, applied as necessary to obtain nonzero values for each of the 128 probabilities.

**23.** For three letters A, B, and C, let the probabilities be

| A | B | C |
|---|---|---|
| .03 | .16 | .81 |

A Huffman code for these monograms is easily determined to be

| A | B | C |
|---|---|---|
| 11 | 10 | 0 |

Confirm that the cost in bits per letter is 1.19. Develop the 9 digrams (AA, AB, ..., CC), their probabilities, and a Huffman code, and determine the cost in bits per digram and bits per letter. Compare the digram and monogram bits-per-letter costs to the minimum of .881 bits-per-letter given by Shannon's Theorem.

One of the most widely used codes in the world is ASCII (the American Standard Code for Information Interchange). It was developed to simplify and standardize machine-to-machine and system-to-system communication. It is a seven-bit code, and all the 128 possible seven-bit combinations are now assigned to provide for the alphabet (both caps and lowercase), the ten decimal digits, and various punctuation marks including three kinds of parentheses, and to ring your "bell," if you have one. (The "bell" is an audible chime or buzzer that is provided on some machines to alert a human operator.) Because the probabilities of the different codes are widely different, considerable savings can be made by Huffman coding. Table 4 lists the ASCII characters. The ASCII code is the 7-bit code for each character determined by the binary equivalent of the decimal row number.

**24.** What is the ASCII code for # ? _____

for + ? _____

for A ? _____

for a ? _____

Using ASCII, how many bits are required to store the word SUPERCALIFRAGILISTICEXPIALIDOCIOUS in upper and lower case letters? _____

As we have seen, for transmitting large amounts of data or text, it frequently pays to compress the information into a smaller number of bits. The same is true for storing information. Compacted data requires fewer bits to store.

**25.** (Optional) Write a computer program for constructing a Huffman code of a source. Use your program and the probabilities given in Table 4 to determine Huffman codes for the ASCII codes.

**26.** (Optional) Using the Huffman code that you constructed in Exercise 25, find the number of bits required to store the word SUPERCALIFRAGILISTICEXPIALIDOCIOUS in upper and lower case letters and compare your answers to the result in Exercise 24.

## D.  Implementations of Huffman Codes

Some computers implement Huffman codes as follows: A text is brought into the computer and stored as ASCII codes. The proportions of each character are determined. The proportions are used as estimates of the probabilities of occurrence, to determine Huffman codes for each character and the text is re-stored as Huffman codes.

As you determined from Exercise 25 (based on an ASCII source), using the conventional Huffman process can lead to long code words. A similar excessive word-length problem arose in designing codes for data transmissions from the LANDSAT program. The LANDSAT satellites return pictures of the terrain over which they pass. They accomplish this by translating a black and white image of the surface below them into a graduated scale of lighter and darker grays. For coding purposes, each gray shade is assigned a number from 0 to 255 where 0=white and 255=black.

A typical system on the satellite sends images to a ground station at a rate of millions of measurements per second. Frequently, data compression can be achieved by sending *differences* between successive samples rather than the samples themselves. The difference is a measure of the direction and amount of change in gray level between successive samples. Therefore, positive as well as negative values are possible. For example, a change from gray level 30 to gray level 50 is a change of +20; but a change from level 50 to level 30 is a change of −20.

Generally, in images of earth scenes, adjacent gray levels are similar, so that small differences occur frequently and large differences occur infrequently. For example, zero differences, which indicate that two successive samples are identical, may occur with probability .25. Differences of ±250, on the other hand, are rare events with typical estimated probability of less than one chance in $10^{20}$. A large difference between two successive samples would mean that the image contained a sudden and sharp contrast within two adjacent image elements (sometimes called *pixels* for picture elements). Such contrasts can happen but are extremely rare.

Hence, the entropy of the *source of sample differences* is generally much smaller than the entropy of the *source of samples*. Accordingly, we know by Shannon's Theorem that sample differences will require fewer bits on the average than the samples themselves.

If the code is to be designed before it is put into use—and it must be!—the exact probabilities of the various source elements cannot be known in advance. To bridge this "data gap," an assumed distribution of probabilities, based on previous experience with similar images, may be used. A distribution frequently observed in gray-level differences has the form:

$$p(0) = (1 - e^{-a}),$$
$$p(x) = \tfrac{1}{2}(1 - e^{-a}) e^{-a|x|} = \tfrac{1}{2} p(0) e^{-a|x|}$$

where $a$ is a constant estimated from available data, and $x$ is the sample difference. For 256 sample gray levels (0, 1, ..., 255), the difference $x$ can vary between −255 and +255.

**27.** Compute the successive differences between the sample gray levels (we give the first three): 54, 54, 54, 55, 55, 54, 0, 255, 100, 255, 0.

Successive differences: 0, 0, 1, _____

We will compare Huffman codes and modified Huffman codes for a smaller example than the LANDSAT case. Suppose the LANDSAT engineers require only 32 gray levels (0, 1, ..., 31). Then the differences can range from −31 to +31.

28. Using the distribution

$$p(0) = .328776, \qquad p(x) = .164388e^{-.398652|x|},$$

compute $p(x)$ for $x = 0, +10, -10, +31, -31$. Express your answers using a power of 10 as in the examples below. (Be sure to round the third digit if necessary.)

$$\text{Example:} \quad p(12) = .0013749 = 137 \times 10^{-5}$$
$$p(0) = .328776 = 329 \times 10^{-3}$$

Note the similarities and differences between the form of our answer and standard scientific notation. For our purposes, it is more convenient not to use decimals.

| $x$ | $p(x)$ |
|-----|--------|
| 0 | _____ |
| +10 | _____ |
| −10 | _____ |
| +31 | _____ |
| −31 | _____ |

Check your answers against Table 5, which contains the $p(x)$ values for $x = 0, \pm 1, \ldots, \pm 31$.

**Table 5**
**Probabilities of Occurrence, Huffman Codes,**
**and Modified Codes For Sample Differences $x$**

for $x = 0, \pm 1, \pm 2, \ldots, \pm 31$

Based on the model:

$$p(x) = \tfrac{1}{2}(1 - e^{-a}) e^{-a|x|}$$

For $a = 0.398652$:

$$p(0) = (1 - e^{-a}) = 0.328776$$

and

$$p(x) = p(-x) = .164388e^{-.398652|x|}.$$

The table gives $p(x)$ values in the form we used for our answers to Exercise 28. We can express this form as

$$p(x) = M \times 10^C$$

where $M$ represents the 3 most significant digits of the calculated $p(x)$ value that would be used to express the number in scientific notation and $C$ is the power of 10. For example, $p(9) = p(-9) = .00455 = 455 \times 10^{-5}$, which is identified in the table by the symbolism 455    − 5.

### Table 5 (cont.)

| ± | $p(x) = p(-x)$ | | Regular Huffman Codes for | |
|---|---|---|---|---|
| x | M | C | Positive x | Negative x |
| 0 | 329 | −3 | 00 | — |
| 1 | 110 | −3 | 101 | 100 |
| 2 | 741 | −4 | 0101 | 0100 |
| 3 | 497 | −4 | 1101 | 1100 |
| 4 | 334 | −4 | 01101 | 01100 |
| 5 | 224 | −4 | 11101 | 11100 |
| 6 | 150 | −4 | 011101 | 011100 |
| 7 | 101 | −4 | 111101 | 111100 |
| 8 | 677 | −5 | 0111101 | 0111100 |
| 9 | 455 | −5 | 1111101 | 1111100 |
| 10 | 305 | −5 | 01111101 | 01111100 |
| 11 | 205 | −5 | 11111101 | 11111100 |
| 12 | 137 | −5 | 011111101 | 011111100 |
| 13 | 923 | −6 | 111111101 | 111111100 |
| 14 | 619 | −6 | 0111111101 | 0111111100 |
| 15 | 416 | −6 | 1111111101 | 1111111100 |
| 16 | 279 | −6 | 01111111101 | 01111111100 |
| 17 | 187 | −6 | 11111111101 | 11111111100 |
| 18 | 126 | −6 | 011111111101 | 011111111100 |
| 19 | 844 | −7 | 111111111101 | 111111111100 |
| 20 | 567 | −7 | 0111111111101 | 0111111111100 |
| 21 | 380 | −7 | 1111111111101 | 1111111111100 |
| 22 | 255 | −7 | 01111111111101 | 01111111111100 |
| 23 | 171 | −7 | 11111111111101 | 11111111111100 |
| 24 | 115 | −7 | 011111111111101 | 011111111111100 |
| 25 | 772 | −8 | 111111111111100 | 011111111111110 |
| 26 | 518 | −8 | 0111111111111110 | 111111111111110 |
| 27 | 348 | −8 | 1111111111111110 | 1111111111111010 |
| 28 | 233 | −8 | 0111111111111111 | 0111111111111110 |
| 29 | 157 | −8 | 1111111111111110 | 1111111111110110 |
| 30 | 105 | −8 | 111111111111101111 | 111111111111101110 |
| 31 | 706 | −9 | 111111111111111111 | 111111111111111110 |

**Table 5 (cont.)**

| ± | $p(x) = p(-x)$ | | Modified Huffman Codes for | |
|---|---|---|---|---|
| x | M | C | **Positive** x | **Negative** x |
| 0 | 329 | −3 | 00 | − |
| 1 | 110 | −3 | 101 | 100 |
| 2 | 741 | −4 | 0101 | 0100 |
| 3 | 497 | −4 | 1101 | 1100 |
| 4 | 334 | −4 | 01101 | 01100 |
| 5 | 224 | −4 | 11101 | 11100 |
| 6 | 150 | −4 | 011101 | 011100 |
| 7 | 101 | −4 | 111101 | 1111000 |
| 8 | 677 | −5 | 0111101 | 0111100 |
| 9 | 455 | −5 | 1111101 | 1111100 |
| 10 | 305 | −5 | 01111101 | 01111100 |
| 11 | 205 | −5 | 11111101 | 11111100 |
| 12 | 137 | −5 | 011111101 | 011111100 |
| 13 | 923 | −6 | 111111101 | 111111100 |
| 14 | 619 | −6 | 0111111101 | 0111111100 |
| 15 | 416 | −6 | 1111111101 | 1111111100 |
| 16 | 279 | −6 | 111100100000 | 111100110000 |
| 17 | 187 | −6 | 111100100001 | 111100110001 |
| 18 | 126 | −6 | 111100100010 | 111100110010 |
| 19 | 844 | −7 | 111100100011 | 111100110011 |
| 20 | 567 | −7 | 111100100100 | 111100110100 |
| 21 | 380 | −7 | 111100100101 | 111100110101 |
| 22 | 255 | −7 | 111100100110 | 111100110110 |
| 23 | 171 | −7 | 111100100111 | 111100110111 |
| 24 | 115 | −7 | 111100101000 | 111100111000 |
| 25 | 772 | −8 | 111100101001 | 111100111001 |
| 26 | 518 | −8 | 111100101011 | 111100111010 |
| 27 | 348 | −8 | 111100101011 | 111100111011 |
| 28 | 233 | −8 | 111100101100 | 111100111100 |
| 29 | 157 | −8 | 111100101101 | 111100111101 |
| 30 | 105 | −8 | 111100101110 | 111100111110 |
| 31 | 706 | −9 | 111100101111 | 111100111111 |

* Observe that −7 requires 7 bits here, but only 6 bits in regular code.

As Table 5 shows, the regular Huffman codes for $x = \pm 31$ are 18 bits long; for a similar source, with $x$ expanded to $\pm 127$, the longest code would exceed 50 bits in length.

# E.  Modified Huffman Codes

These long code words can create timing and storage problems for the coder and decoder. One available solution is to use a *modified* Huffman code, which gives up a little efficiency in order to shorten the longer codes. In a modified code, elements having a probability less than some chosen threshold are represented by a distinctive prefix code, followed by a binary number representation of the element—or the gray level, in the picture problem.

A modified Huffman code has been proposed for the LANDSAT imaging problem. On the third page of Table 5, we show a modified version of the regular Huffman code, which is on the second page of that table. The modified code is created by the following steps: (1) the regular codes for $\pm 16$ through $\pm 31$ are discarded; (2) the regular code 111100 for $-7$ is discarded, and in its place is substituted 1111000 (neither this code, nor 1111001, is a prefix of any of the remaining regular codes for 0 to $\pm 15$); (3) the values $\pm 16$ to $\pm 31$ inclusive are now coded by the distinctive prefix 1111001, plus a sign bit, plus four bits representing the numbers 1 to 16 (as 0000 through 1111). The choice of $-7$ as the code to be extended was arbitrary in this example; it cuts the longest codes from 18 bits down to 12. The loss in efficiency for modified Huffman codes comes about mainly through adding one bit to the code for $-7$; the time lost thereby is not regained by shortening the longer codes. By adding a bit to $-3$, instead of $-7$, and thus making a shorter distinctive prefix available, we would cut the modified codes to ten bits, matching those for the longest remaining regular codes—at a greater cost in efficiency.

29. For the distribution in Table 5

   a. How long would a fixed-length code for these data have to be?

   b. (Optional) Using the computer program that you wrote for computing entropy (Exercise 19), calculate the shortest attainable average bit length according to Shannon's Theorem. (Remember that $x$ has 31 positive values, 31 negative values, and one zero value—a total of 63 values.)

   c. (Optional) Using the computer program that you wrote for computing average code word length (Exercise 21), calculate the expected bit length for both the regular Huffman code and the modified Huffman code given in Table 5.

   d. Approximately, how much would the expected bit length increase, if the code for $-3$ had been increased by one bit, instead of the code for $-7$?

We should remark that adaptive coding systems now exist that will revise and improve an initial makeshift distribution, as experience accumulates regarding the actual frequencies of the elements in the source.

Congratulations! You have learned the concepts of coding, code "costs," uniquely decodable, prefix property, decoding, source, source probabilities, independent source, entropy, Shannon's Theorem, digrams, trigrams, Huffman and modified Huffman codes, ASCII characters, and adaptive coding. Get ready for some additional interesting concepts in Part II.

# Part II
# ERROR CONTROL CODING

In Part I, we focussed on efficiency of transmission. But efficiency buys nothing if the message is garbled along the way, and so in this part, we focus on reliability. The demand for efficient (speedy) yet reliable data transmission and storage systems has been accentuated in recent years by the emergence of large-scale, high-speed data networks for the exchange, processing, and storing of more and more types of information in virtually all walks of life. A merging of communications and computer technology is required in the design of these systems. A major concern of the designer is the control of errors so that reliable reproduction of data can be obtained.

Communication links include telephone lines, high frequency radio links, telemetry links, microwave links, and satellite links. Typical storage techniques include core and semiconductor memories, magnetic tapes, drums, discs, optical memory units, and so on. Each of these is subject to disturbances. On a telephone line the disturbance may be from switching noise, thermal noise, crosstalk, or lightning. On a storage medium surface, defects or dust are prime sources of undesirable noise.

## A. Parity Check

A simple but widely used method for detecting single errors—that is, a bit changed from a 0 to a 1 or a 1 to a 0—is to append one bit (called a parity bit) to each code word so that the number of 1's in the code word, including the parity bit, is an even number. As a simple example, consider the following 16-element gray level code:

| Gray Level | Binary String | Gray Level | Binary String |
|---|---|---|---|
| 0 | 0000 | 8 | 1000 |
| 1 | 0001 | 9 | 1001 |
| 2 | 0010 | 10 | 1010 |
| 3 | 0011 | 11 | 1011 |
| 4 | 0100 | 12 | 1100 |
| 5 | 0101 | 13 | 1101 |
| 6 | 0110 | 14 | 1110 |
| 7 | 0111 | 15 | 1111 |

The parity bit for gray level 5 will be a 0 (not shown above), since the code word has an even number of 1's. The extended code word is 01010, the last bit being the parity bit.

**30.** What are the parity bits and extended codes for

|  | Parity Bit | Extended Code |
|---|---|---|
| Gray level 2? | _____ | _____ |
| Gray level 3? | _____ | _____ |

Gray level 7? _____  _____

**31.** What are the parity bits and extended codes for the seven-bit ASCII characters (Table 4) #, +, A, a?

|   | **Parity Bit** | **Extended Code** |
|---|---|---|
| # | _____ | _____ |
| + | _____ | _____ |
| A | _____ | _____ |
| a | _____ | _____ |

If one bit is changed during transmission, the number of 1's in the received character will have the wrong parity and the receiver will know an error has occurred. For example, suppose the extended gray level code 01110 was received. It has three 1's (an odd number) so you know an error has occurred and you would ask for the code word to be retransmitted.

**32.** Which of the following received extended ASCII codes are in error?

| **Received Code** | **In Error (Yes or No)** |
|---|---|
| 11000011 | _____ |
| 11000110 | _____ |
| 10000000 | _____ |

We assumed that 11000110 was correct because it had even parity (an even number of 1's). If at most one error occurred, we would be right. If the code word were 10000010 and the second and sixth bits were altered to 1's during the transmission, we would be wrong. We would not have detected the error.

Likewise, if the parity bit and another bit were both wrong, the error would pass undetected; if the parity bit only was in error, a false alarm would occur. But as double errors are far less frequent than single errors, the single parity bit drastically reduces the undetected error rate.

**33.** Decode the extended code ASCII message: 10010011010000001001 1001100111111010111010001011010000011011001010011111101 01010. _____

In practice, the parity bit check is used when the error probability for the alteration of a bit is very small. Otherwise, single parity checks give unacceptable results.

Techniques for controlling data-transmission errors involve both the detection and correction of errors. Some codes can only detect that an error has occurred while others can also correct errors. When a code with a good error-detection capability is used, a request for retransmission is given whenever an error is detected. However, with an error-correction code, the code determines the error location and the correction. When the receiver detects errors in such a code, it attempts to determine the error locations and corrects the errors. If the exact locations of errors are determined, the received code word will be correctly decoded; if the receiver fails to determine the exact location of errors, the received code word will be decoded incorrectly and the erroneous data will be given to the user. There are also hybrid systems in which failure to locate an error triggers a request for retransmission.

# B. *K*-redundant Codes

Another approach to error control is simple redundancy coding. For an example, let's return to the 16 gray levels:

| Gray Level | Binary String | Gray Level | Binary String |
|---|---|---|---|
| 0 | 0000 | 8 | 1000 |
| 1 | 0001 | 9 | 1001 |
| 2 | 0010 | 10 | 1010 |
| 3 | 0011 | 11 | 1011 |
| 4 | 0100 | 12 | 1100 |
| 5 | 0101 | 13 | 1101 |
| 6 | 0110 | 14 | 1110 |
| 7 | 0111 | 15 | 1111 |

You could transmit gray level 3 as 000000111111, a 12-bit word where each of the original bits has been replaced by three bits. That is, each 0 is replaced by 000 and each 1 is replaced by 111. This is called a 3-redundant code.

34. What are the 3-redundant codes for gray levels 4 and 7?

| Gray level | 3-redundant codes |
|---|---|
| 4 | _____ |
| 7 | _____ |

You could use the following decoding scheme:
If 000 or 001 or 010 or 100 is received, decode the triplet as a 0.
If 110 or 101 or 011 or 111 is received, decode the triplet as a 1.
This particular decoding is called majority vote decoding.

35. Decode the following 3-redundant gray level code words by majority vote decoding.

    a. 010110000111 _____

    b. 100101111011 _____

In the example above, suppose the probability of error for each bit is 1/5, an intolerably high value. And suppose the noise (interference) affects each transmitted symbol independently.

36. Compute the probability that a 3-bit code word will be sent without error via a memoryless channel[1] with an error probability for a single bit of

    a. 1/5 _____

    b. 1/10 _____

---

[1]The word *channel* is used in information theory as a generic term for a transmission medium. Typical transmission channels include telephone lines, high frequency radio links, microwave links, and so on. A channel for which the noise affects each transmitted symbol independently is called a *memoryless* channel. For such a channel, the success probability for a code word is the product of the success probabilities for each bit. For example, suppose the bit error probability is 1/5. Then the probability that 1011 will be sent correctly is $4/5 \times 4/5 \times 4/5 \times 4/5 = 256/625$ or .41.

   **c.** 1/20 _____

   **d.** 1/100 _____

With 3-redundancy coding and majority vote decoding, message errors can still occur. If 000 is submitted to the channel and 000 or 001 or 010 or 100 is received, you will correctly interpret that a 0 bit was intended. With a bit-error probability of 1/5 for a memoryless channel, the probability of receiving

$$000 \text{ is } 4/5 \times 4/5 \times 4/5 = 64/125;$$
$$001 \text{ is } 4/5 \times 4/5 \times 1/5 = 16/125;$$
$$010 \text{ is } 4/5 \times 1/5 \times 4/5 = 16/125;$$
$$100 \text{ is } 1/5 \times 4/5 \times 4/5 = 16/125.$$

Hence, the probability of receiving a 000 or 001 or 010 or 100 if a 000 is input to the channel is the sum

$$64/125 + 16/125 + 16/125 + 16/125 = 112/125 = .896.$$

Now if we use 9 bits to send a 3-bit code, the probability of correct transmission is $.896 \times .896 \times .896 = .719$. Observe the improvement over the result in Exercise 36a.

   **37.** If the 3-redundancy code 111 is submitted to a memoryless channel with bit-error probability of 1/5, what is the probability of correctly inferring that a 1 was sent using majority vote decoding? _____

With a bit-error probability of 1/5, the probability of correctly majority vote decoding a 3-redundancy code is 112/125. Hence the probability of correctly decoding a 4-bit gray level code, which is submitted to the channel as a 12-bit word (using 3-redundancy coding) is the product $112/125 \times 112/125 \times 112/125 \times 112/125 = 0.64$. This is an improvement over the .41 success rate without redundancy. Also the probability-of-error per bit dropped from 1/5 to about $(1/10)(13/125)$.

   **38.** Compute the probability-of-error per information-bit using

   5-redundancy. _____

If you were to use 17-redundancy, the probability-of-error per bit would drop to less than .01. Using higher and higher redundancy coding you could reduce the error as close to zero as you like, but only at the expense of reducing the rate of transmission in information-bits/bits-sent. In summary, you have

| Redundancy | Probability-of-error/ information-bit | Rate (information-bits/ bits-sent) |
|---|---|---|
| 0 | 0.20 | 1 |
| 3 | 0.10 | 0.33 |
| 5 | 0.06 | 0.20 |
| 17 | 0.01 | 0.06 |

It would appear that in order to keep pushing the error probability to zero, you must keep pushing the rate of information transmission down to zero.

Fortunately, this is not true, as you will discover after we explore several other ways of controlling for errors.

In the case of a 3-redundant code, it's obvious that information is coming through at a rate no greater than one-third the rate of bit transmission. The ratio of information bits to total bits sent is called the *information transmission rate,* and in this context the phrase is often abbreviated to "transmission rate," or even to "rate."

A single-bit error probability of 1/5 for a memoryless channel is not realistic. More common values in practice are 1/10 or 1/100 or 1/1000. Suppose a bit error probability of 1/1000 was not quite acceptable for sending 4-bit gray levels and you were striving for a decrease in error rate without much reducing the transmission rate (information-bits/bits-sent). You could use a popular single-error-correcting code. This code has the capability of detecting and correcting one error among 12 information bits by transmitting 20 bits, eight of which are redundant.

To illustrate the code we let the 12 information bits be three successively transmitted 4-bit gray level codes, say gray levels 3 (0011), 9 (1001), and 13 (1101), arranged in rows of an array:

    0011

    1001

    1101

We append to each row and each column one more bit (a parity bit), chosen to make the number of ones in each row and column even. We also add a symbol at the lower right corner, chosen to make the last row also have an even number of ones. For the example the expanded array is:

    00110

    10010

    11011

    01111

39. Find the parity checks for the gray level codes 4, 5, 6 given below:

    0100

    0101

    0110

If an entire array (including the parity checks) is transmitted row by row (or column by column) and if there is a single error (a 1 changed to a 0 or a 0 changed to a 1), it can be corrected. Correction is done by checking each row and column for an even number of 1's. If there is a single error, one column and one row will have an odd number of 1's. The error is at the intersection, and it can be corrected by changing the 0 to a 1 or vice versa.

40. The following received array contains one error. Circle it.

    11001

    01010

    01100

    01111

You can think of the 20 symbols of the expanded array as a code word. This code has $n = 20$ bits, of which $k = 12$ are information bits. It is referred to as a (20, 12) code. There are $n - k = 8$ check bits. These are the redundant bits added to provide the code word with error-correcting capability. The transmission rate, $r$, for the (20, 12) code is $r = k/n = 12/20$. Most error-correcting codes for memoryless channels are based on parity check ideas like the (20, 12) code. However, the ideas generally are mathematically deeper and lead to better codes. For example, Hamming codes, discussed next, require the least number of check bits for a single-error-correcting code, significantly fewer than the (20, 12) code.

## C.  Hamming Codes

The error-correcting method given in this section was devised by Richard Hamming and is known as a Hamming code. We illustrate a Hamming code for the gray level example:

| Gray Level | Binary String | Gray Level | Binary String |
|------------|---------------|------------|---------------|
| 0          | 0000          | 8          | 1000          |
| 1          | 0001          | 9          | 1001          |
| 2          | 0010          | 10         | 1010          |
| 3          | 0011          | 11         | 1011          |
| 4          | 0100          | 12         | 1100          |
| 5          | 0101          | 13         | 1101          |
| 6          | 0110          | 14         | 1110          |
| 7          | 0111          | 15         | 1111          |

In this example, three parity-check bits are added to each four-bit gray level code to form a new word of seven bits. The seven bits are numbered from one to seven starting with the left-most bit. The bit numbers 1, 2, and 4 are parity-check bits. The remaining bits are information bits. Each parity bit checks specific bit positions and *the parity bit is chosen so that the number of 1's in the checked positions is even.* The bit positions checked by the parity bits are

Bit 1 checks bits 1, 3, 5, 7;

Bit 2 checks bits 2, 3, 6, 7;

Bit 4 checks bits 4, 5, 6, 7.

The general rule is that bit $x$ is checked by the bit positions that sum to $x$. For example, bit 5 is checked by bit positions 1 and 4. The gray level code 6 is represented by 0110. Its Hamming code is <u>110</u>0<u>1</u>10. The underscored bits are check bits. Note that the number of 1's in bit positions 1, 3, 5, 7 is even; the same is true for bit positions 2, 3, 6, 7 and 4, 5, 6, 7.

**41.** For gray level 9, the information bits of a (7, 4) Hamming code are

$$\underline{\_\_1\_001}$$
$$\text{1 2 3 4 5 6 7}$$

After the check bits are filled in by the rule given above, we have the complete Hamming code:

$$\underline{0011001}$$
$$\text{1 2 3 4 5 6 7}$$

For gray level 12, the information bits are:

$$\underline{\phantom{0}}\ \underline{\phantom{0}}\ \underline{1}\ \underline{\phantom{0}}\ \underline{1}\ \underline{0}\ \underline{0}$$
$$1\ 2\ 3\ 4\ 5\ 6\ 7$$

Fill in the check bits, and also, construct the Hamming codes for gray levels 5 and 14.

The Hamming code for gray level 6 is 1100110. Consider what would happen if the third bit were altered by noise during transmission. The received word would be 1110110. The 3 parity checks would be determined by the receiver. The two checks containing bit 3 would be incorrect, indicating that either bit 3 or bit 7 (the bits common to the two checks) is incorrect. But the parity check involving bits 4, 5, 6, 7 was correct so bit 7 is correct. Consequently, the incorrect bit must be bit 3. So the receiver could change bit 3 from a 1 to a 0, thereby reconstructing the original code.

42. The received code 1101110 is a Hamming code for some gray level with one bit in error. Find the bit which is in error and determine the gray level which was transmitted. _____

_____

43. The following received codes either contain no errors or a single error. Determine the gray level that each represents.

| Received code | Gray level |
| --- | --- |
| a. 0101010 | _____ |
| b. 0001010 | _____ |
| c. 1110110 | _____ |
| d. 1010110 | _____ |

The Hamming code we have been using is a (7, 4) code. Three parity-check bits are required to correct a single error in the four information bits.

An erroneous bit in a (7, 4) Hamming code can be quickly found by constructing a three-digit binary number called *the syndrome*. We will illustrate the syndrome by applying it to Exercise 43c. The *first* check in that problem showed an error in bit 1, 3, 5, or 7, so the *last* digit in the syndrome is 1. The *second* check showed an error in bit 2, 3, 6, or 7, so the *second-last* digit in the syndrome is also a 1. The *third* check showed no error in bits 4, 5, 6, or 7, so the *third-last* digit in the syndrome is 0; and the syndrome is therefore 011. This is the number 3, in the binary notation, so the error is indicated to be in the third digit, as we found before. The syndrome will locate an error in any one of the seven positions, including the check positions, provided that there is only a single error.

44. Use the syndrome to verify the answers to Exercises 43a, b, d.

45. What is the transmission rate, $r$, for the (7, 4) Hamming code?

_____

The (7, 4) code is only one example of a Hamming code. The same error-finding principle can be extended to longer codes, and the beauty of the scheme is that the transmission rate goes up as the code gets longer. In a 31-bit code, a 5-bit syndrome will pinpoint a single error anywhere in the string, and the resulting (31, 26) Hamming code has a transmission rate of .84, which is quite an improvement over the .57 rate of the (7, 4) code.

Error-correcting codes are widely used to improve the reliability of computer storage. The IBM system 7030, built in 1961, was the first IBM system to use a Hamming code for its core memory. In the 1970s, semiconductor memories replaced core memories. They are faster than core memories, but less reliable. As a result, the use of error-correcting codes for improving semiconductor memory has become a standard design feature.

**46.** Develop an (11, 7) Hamming code to detect and correct a single error in 7-bit ASCII code words.

Exercise 46 was intended to show the complexity of devising efficient single-error-correcting codes. You may have used trial and error. The problem gets more complicated in the development of efficient codes for correcting multiple errors, especially when the information bit strings are long (over ten bits). Some of the most efficient codes are based on algebraic concepts like groups, fields, vector spaces, and Galois fields. These techniques have led to the discovery, for example, of

1. Single-error-correcting Hamming codes for information bit strings of length 3, 7, 15, 31, ..., in fact of any length $n = 2^m - 1$ for $m \geq 2$.

2. The (23/12) Golay code. This code is capable of correcting any combination of three or fewer random errors in a string of 23 bits. Since its discovery by Golay in 1949, it has become a subject of study by many mathematicians because of its beautiful algebraic structure. The code has also been used for error-correction on the Voyager spacecraft and several other communication systems.

3. Reed-Solomon codes. These important and useful codes are very sophisticated. The IBM photodigital mass storage system known as Digital Cypress uses a (61, 50) shortened Reed-Solomon code. It is capable of correcting multiple errors. Reed-Solomon codes are used in the communication links of many space programs.

## D. Burst-Error-Correcting Codes

So far in this chapter, we have discussed coding methods for correcting random transmission errors. That is, each transmitted bit is affected independently by noise. However, there are many communication channels which are affected by disturbances that cause transmission errors to occur in clusters. For example, on telephone or television lines, a stroke of lightning or an electrical disturbance can affect tens, hundreds, or thousands of consecutive bits. On magnetic tapes, dust, scratches, or defects can cause clusters of errors. Such clusters are called burst errors, and codes to correct them are called burst-error-correcting codes.

Suppose the Space Telescope is sending to Earth the following sequence of 10 gray levels during a brief period of transmission: 7, 6, 7, 7, 8, 7, 6, 8,

8, 8. The Hamming codes are:

0001111
1100110
0001111
0001111
1110000
0001111
1100110
1110000
1110000
1110000

During the transmission of the first gray level 8 (the fifth row in the array), radio frequency interference from an unidentified satellite causes all of the bits in the fifth row to be incorrectly transmitted, so that 0001111 is received instead of 1110000. As a receiver you would be unaware of the burst error and incorrectly interpret 0001111 as gray level 7.

Can you think of a way to correct burst errors? The key idea is simple but extremely clever and is based on the concept of "distributing the burst errors over many code words." This is done by transmitting the code array column by column rather than row by row. The resulting code is called an *interleaved* code.  Hence the array above would be transmitted in column order and would look like this if the transmission were free of error:

0100101111          0100101111          0000100111
COLUMN 1            COLUMN 2            COLUMN 3

1011010000          1111011000          1111011000
COLUMN 4            COLUMN 5            COLUMN 6

1011010000
COLUMN 7

With the transmission in column order, the burst error would have affected only one bit of seven different code words rather than seven bits of one code word.  The bits affected are the *29th to the 35th bits transmitted.*  In the display above, these bits are underlined. As the bits are received, you could put them back into row order by appropriate sorting. After the first 28 bits have been received, the sort looks like this:

000
110
000
000
111
000
110
11
11

The next seven bits are incorrectly transmitted. So after the first 35 bits are transmitted the sort looks like this:

000<u>0</u>

110<u>1</u>

000<u>0</u>

000<u>0</u>

111<u>1</u>

000

110

11<u>0</u>

11<u>0</u>

When all bits have been transmitted, we are back to our original array except for the seven incorrectly transmitted bits:

000<u>0</u>111

110<u>1</u>110

000<u>0</u>111

000<u>0</u>111

111<u>1</u>000

0001111

1100110

11<u>0</u>0000

11<u>0</u>0000

Finally, the single error in each row is detected and corrected by the parity checks originally assigned.

Interleaved Hamming codes are used in the U.S. Army TACFIRE computer system. TACFIRE encodes messages of seven-bit ASCII characters by a $(12,7)$ Hamming code. Then it interleaves 16 of these code words. Hence it is capable of correcting a single error burst, 16 bits long, every $16 \times 12$ bits in the message. Like the $(11,7)$ Hamming code, it can correct a single random error in a seven-bit block. The extra bit in the $(12,7)$ code adds the capability of detecting two errors (see Appendix I).

The Space Telescope system uses interleaved Reed-Solomon codes to provide the capability of correcting an error burst of 500 bits. It is not surprising that this code can handle virtually all errors due to weather conditions and radio frequency interference. However, error bursts longer than 1000 bits can arise from a problem called cycle slip, a problem which remains the most pressing issue to be resolved in the Space Telescope system.

## E. Application of Error-Correcting Codes to the Compact Disc Digital Audio System

In 1877, Edison's phonograph played the nursery rhyme "Mary had a little lamb," after he had recorded it on a wax cylinder in his own voice: the human voice had been reproduced for the first time. Then came Berliner's wax disc, followed by the 78 rpm shellac disc, and ultimately the modern long-play record. Frequently when we enjoy our LPs at home, the music is almost perfectly reproduced by hi-fi equipment. A serious drawback of these records is that they have to be very carefully handled if the quality is to be preserved. The mechanical tracking of the stylus in the grooves in the record causes wear. This wear, together with dust, scratches, and defects on the record surface, often produces undesirable sounds. Such problems are less troublesome with the compact disc. It is read optically, so playing it cannot produce any damage, and dust and fingermarks have little effect—because errors can be corrected. The compact disc also differs from the long-play record in that the sound is recorded in digital form. What does digital mean? Why is digital better?

Sounds that our ears can hear and our brains can interpret can be plotted as smooth curves such as:

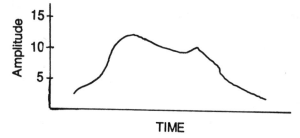

These curves indicate the "loudness" or amplitude of soundwaves over time. We say such sounds are analog signals. A sound wave is a sequence of pulsations, like ripples on a pond. It has amplitude and frequency; that is, the ripples may be deep or shallow, and the peaks may be close together or far apart. These properties are continuously variable; the strength of the magnetic field impressed on a recording tape also varies in wavelike fashion, with continuously variable amplitude and frequency. Analog recordings, generally, are based on continuously variable physical properties of the recording medium.

Another way to represent sounds is with a sequence of numbers. To obtain the numbers, we measure the strength of the analog signal at regular intervals of time. These measurements are indicated by the vertical lines in the drawing below:

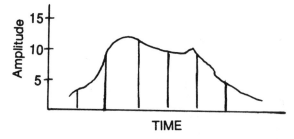

In this example the sequence of numbers (amplitudes) was rounded off to integers, 3, 10, 12, 10, 9, 5. This sequence of numbers contains *some* of the information in the analog signal. The analog signal can be approximated better and better by increasing the sampling frequency (including more amplitude values per unit time in the sampling sequence), and by rounding the amplitude to tenths or hundredths or further, rather than integers. These re-

**E. Application of Error-Correcting Codes to the Compact Disc Digital Audio System**

finements can provide an amplitude sequence (called a digital representation) that matches the sound quality of a good analog recording.

Below the surface of a compact disc itself, music is stored as a sequence of binary numbers (representing amplitudes), which are physically written as sequences of microscopic "bumps" 0.16 millionths of a meter high and 0.6 millionths of a meter wide. A 1 is represented as the beginning or end of a bump and a 0 as an area where there is no change. The beam of light from a laser is focussed on the bumps, and the changes in the reflected beam as it passes over them are sensed by electronic circuits which interpret the 1's and 0's and perform actual computations with these numbers in order to prepare the signal for human ears. A covering layer of transparent plastic protects the bumps against wear.

## Combatting the Noise

Representing the sounds as sequences of numbers provides the means of combatting noise. In the compact disc system, the binary information is protected against errors (caused by defects on the surface or dust or scratches) by adding parity checks in the form of Reed-Solomon codes. Because the errors are mostly burst-like, interleaving is used to spread the errors out over a longer time.

# Appendix I

# HAMMING's (12,7) SEC-DED CODE

To obtain a single-error-correcting (SEC) code plus a double-error-detecting (DED) code you begin with a single-error-correcting code. To this code you add one more position for checking all previous positions, using an even parity check.

For example, in Exercise 46 you used an (11,7) single-error-correcting code to code the 7-character ASCII code for the exclamation point. That code was 01011001001.

The (12,7) code for ! is 01011001001$\underline{1}$. The underscored 1 provides an even parity check on the entire code.

To see the operation of this code, you have to examine three possibilities:

1. No errors occur in transmission. In this case all parity checks including the last are satisfied.

2. A single error occurs in transmission. In this case the last parity check always fails whether the error be in the information, the original check position, or the last check position. The original check bits give the position of the error. If the 4 original checks show no error, the error must be in the last check position.

3. Two errors occur in transmission. In all such situations the last parity check is satisfied, while the original checks indicate some kind of error.

**A.1.** All of the following received (12,7) Hamming codes are for the 7-bit ASCII codes. Each received code has either 0, 1, or 2 errors. Determine which and decode (find the ASCII symbol) for the 0 or 1 error cases.

   **a.** 010110010011 _____

   **b.** 111110010011 _____

   **c.** 010110010010 _____

# Appendix II
# SUGGESTED READINGS

Gallager, R., Variations on a Theme by Huffman. *IEEE Transactions on Information Theory*, Vol. IT-24, No. 6, November 1978, pp. 668–674.

Gilbert, E., Information Theory After 18 Years. *Science*, Vol. 152, 15 April 1966, pp. 320–325.

Hamming, R., Error Detecting and Correcting Codes. *The Bell System Technical Journal*, Vol. 29, No. 147, April 1950, pp. 147–160.

Harris, A., et. al., Space Telescope: End-to-End Data System Study. Final Report for the National Aeronautics and Space Administration. Internal Report of Science Applications, Inc., 3 Preston Street, Bedford, Mass. 01730, June 1981.

Hawkes, C., Firstenberg, A., Final Report on Data Compression Techniques. Prepared for National Aeronautics and Space Administration, Rockwell International Report MRDC 41102.36 FR, September 1983.

Hoeve, J., Timmermans, J., and Vries, L., Error Correction and Concealment in the Compact Disc System. *Philips Technical Review*, Vol. 40, No. 6, 1982, pp. 166–172.

Huffman, D., A Method for the Construction of Minimum-Redundancy Codes. *Proceedings of the IRE (Institute Radio Engineers)* 40, (1952), pp. 1098–1101.

Kohlahse, C., The Voyager Uranus Travel Guide. Jet Propulsion Laboratory Internal Report JPL-D-2580 for National Aeronautics and Space Administration, August 5, 1985.

Peek, J., Communication Aspects of the Compact Disc Digital Audio Systems. *IEEE Communications Magazine*, Vol. 23, No. 2, February 1985, pp. 7–15.

Rogers, H., Information Theory. *Mathematics Magazine*, March 1964, pp. 63–78.

Shannon, C., The Mathematical Theory of Communication. *Bell System Technical Journal*, Vol. 27, (1948), pp. 379–423; 623–656.

# Appendix III

# COMPUTER PROJECTS

Write computer programs for:

1. Constructing a Huffman code of a source, if you haven't already done so in Exercise 25. Use this program to code 4-grams and 5-grams for the source probabilities 0.7 and 0.3. Compare your average code word lengths with Exercises 17 and 18.

2. Processing ASCII characters as they are entered into a computer (say in a word processing application), counting the frequencies of each character, coding the character by a Huffman code, and storing the codes.

3. Hamming coding and decoding of a 7-bit source subject to random errors.

4. Hamming coding and decoding of a 7-bit source subject to burst-errors of length 8.

# Appendix IV

# CLAUDE SHANNON: FATHER OF INFORMATION THEORY

Claude Elwood Shannon, the father of Information Theory, was born in Gaylord, Michigan on April 30, 1916. He received his B.S. degree from the University of Michigan in 1936. In 1939 he became a Bowles Fellow at the Massachusetts Institute of Technology, and was awarded his M.S. and Ph.D. there a year later. Shannon developed his remarkable theory in the 1940s as the culmination of several years of research at Bell Laboratories in Murray Hill, New Jersey.

Information theory is the mathematical treatment of problems that arise in the storage and transmission of information. We receive information everyday, such as a telephone number, the name of a new neighbor, or the cost of a new car. Such information is stored somewhere (in the brain or in a notebook, for instance) and later transmitted in some manner. To use, or transmit, information, it is often necessary to transform it. In telegraphy, the letters of the text are replaced by codes; in television, the image is converted into signals transmitted by electromagnetic waves. In order to treat such problems mathematically, we need to have a quantitative measure of information.

Shannon investigated the concepts of "communication," "information," and "message," and defined a communication system as one consisting of the following components: an information source, which selected the message to be sent; a transmitter, which encoded the message; the signal resulting from the encoding; a communication channel for the message; a receiver, which decoded the message; and finally, a destination, which was analogous to the source. He recognized that noise of external origin, consisting of unintentional and undesirable variations in the received signal, was an ever-present problem.

Shannon brought the second law of thermodynamics into play, and drew an analogy between entropy (degree of randomness) and information. In his definition, information does not refer to the meaningful content of a particular message, but to the degree of freedom with which a source may choose among elements to compose the desired message. For example, suppose the message "QZWXL" came to us over a wire, and we knew that each letter had a definite, distinct meaning, which we could look up in a code book. It would then be disastrous if noise caused the message to be changed to "QZWXC." The English language is a less random environment. In "the cow gumped over the moon," the error is not so critical.

Shannon's work proved to have far-reaching implications, not only in the technical and engineering aspects of communication systems, but also in music, art, psychology, physics, and medicine. Finding optimal codings for various messages is an interesting application of communication theory. However, it is but one aspect of the total study of communication: information contained within language, symbol, and gesture.

Especially noteworthy among Shannon's early contributions was his 1938 paper "A Symbolic Analysis of Relay and Switching Circuits," in which he made clear the direct relationship between the binary values "0" and "1" and the two "truth values" of Boolean algebra.

Dr. Shannon remained at Bell Laboratories until 1958, when he became Donner Professor of Science at MIT. He has received numerous professional honors, including election to the National Academy of Science in 1956. He also received the Ballantine Medal from the Franklin Institute in 1955, and honorary degrees from Yale and Princeton Universities. Perhaps his finest accolade came from the Russian mathematician A. I. Khinchin, who said: "Rarely does it happen that a new discipline (information theory) achieves the character of a mature and disciplined scientific theory in the first investigation devoted to it."

# Appendix V

# PROOF THAT THE HUFFMAN CODE GIVES MINIMUM REDUNDANCY

There are thousands of words in the dictionary, but only 26 letters in the alphabet. This simple fact illustrates the principle that a large collection of elements (the hundreds of thousands of words in the English language) can be conveniently represented by combinations of a small collection of coding symbols (the 26 letters of the alphabet).

In binary coding, which is the only kind we shall consider here, we use only the two symbols 0 and 1. If we wish to construct a code for the transmission of messages in the English language, the first question to be considered is whether we shall have a different code for every word in the dictionary (with thousands of different codes), or a different code for every letter in the alphabet (with only 26 different codes). Obviously, the second is the simpler choice, and if we take that approach, the alphabet is the *source*, the 26 letters are the *elements*, and the 26 different strings of 0's and 1's by which we code the letters are called the *element codes* or *code words*. The 0's and 1's are called *coding symbols, digits,* or *bits*. We cannot decipher a coded message without a *key* that links each digit string to the letter that it represents: for example, a two-column table with the elements in one column, and the code words in the other column, each opposite the corresponding element. Such a table of related code words and elements is often called *the code*; we shall be a little more formal here, and call it the *source code*.

An important basic fact, of which Huffman coding seeks to take advantage, is that in many sources, some elements will appear more frequently than others in a typical message. For example, it's well known that E and T are among the commonest letters in the English language, and that Q and Z appear much less frequently. Thus we may be able to shorten the average length of an element code by using short strings of coding symbols for the frequent elements, and longer strings for the rare ones.

How can we get the maximum savings out of this tactic?

Let's spell out Huffman's problem in more detail:

> Given a source of $N$ elements (for example, 32 gray levels or the ten digits of the decimal number system), the relative frequencies or probabilities of the elements, and two coding symbols, the digits 0 and 1, how can we construct a code in which the average length of a code word is minimized?    (1)

A basic assumption of the problem, as yet unstated, is that each bit takes the same time to be transmitted, whether it is a 0 or a 1, so that the time taken to transmit a message is directly proportional to the number of digits in it.

Let

$$P(i) = \text{ the probability of the } i\text{-th element.} \qquad (2)$$

As there are only $N$ elements in the source, these probabilities must add up to unity:

$$P(1) + P(2) + \cdots + P(N) = \sum_{i=1}^{N} P(i) = 1. \qquad (3)$$

Let

$$L(i) = \text{ the number of bits in the } i\text{-th element code,} \qquad (4)$$

and let

$$ACL = \text{ the average element code length.} \qquad (5)$$

Then

$$ACL = \sum_{i=1}^{N} P(i)L(i). \qquad (6)$$

The $ACL$ as shown in (6) is a weighted average, in which the more probable elements weigh more heavily in determining the average element code length.

Let's return for a moment to the alphabet coding example. Suppose we have constructed a code in which the bit strings are not all the same length. Now we wish to know what the average bit length of a coded element will be if we use our code to transmit English text. So we pick up the daily newspaper, the *New York Times* or the *Toledo Blade* or whatever's available, and we tally letters from randomly chosen articles until we have counted a large number of them; and we let that number be $M$. We then compute:

$$ACL = \frac{n(A)L(A) + n(B)L(B) + \cdots + n(Z)L(Z)}{M}, \qquad (7)$$

where

$$n(A) = \text{ the number of } A\text{'s in our sample, and}$$
$$L(A) = \text{ the number of bits in the } A \text{ code, and}$$
$$n(B) = \text{ the number of } B\text{'s in the sample, and so on.}$$

(7) can be written

$$ACL = L(A)n(A)/M + L(B)n(B)/M + \cdots + L(Z)n(Z)/M. \qquad (8)$$

Now, in the first term on the right-hand side of (8), the factor $n(A)/M$ is the relative frequency of $A$'s in our sample, and if $M$ is large, it is a good estimate of $p(A)$, which is the probability that any letter, chosen at random from the *Times* or *Blade* as the case may be, will be an $A$. Hence we can make a substitution in (8) to obtain

$$ACL = L(A)p(A) + L(B)p(B) + \cdots + L(Z)p(Z). \qquad (9)$$

Now, compare (9) and (6), and you will see that the two forms are equivalent.

The objective of Huffman coding is to make the $ACL$ as small as possible for the given $N$ values of $P(i)$; if this objective is achieved, the coding is said to be *optimum*, and the code is said to have *minimum redundancy*.

## A. The Five Requirements for an Optimum Code

The first two restrictions on the code are these:

> **Restriction** (a)   No two element codes will be identical bit for bit.   (10)

> **Restriction** (b)   The element codes will be constructed in such a way that no additional indication is necessary to specify where an element code begins and ends, once the starting point of a sequence of element codes is known.   (11)

If Restriction (a) above is not satisfied, it will be impossible to tell the two identically coded elements apart.

Restriction (b) is imposed to meet the basic requirement that we must have some way to tell where one element code ends, and the next one begins. Line 11 doesn't tell exactly how to do that, but the mystery will clear up shortly.

There are several ways to tell where element codes end. If the element codes are all the same length, that solves the problem. But in Huffman coding, our purpose is to reduce the average code length by making some codes shorter than others, so that way is barred.

A second way might be to supply the "additional information" that Restriction (b) forbids—that is, to devise a special end-of-element code (EOC) to tell us where one element ends and the next begins. This special code would have to be inserted after every element—that is, after every letter in an alphabetic transmission—and its effect would be to lengthen the transmission, rather than shorten it. Thus it seems unlikely that a code using EOC's could equal the efficiency of a code that doesn't need them.

The third way of signalling where an element code ends is the *Prefix Property*, which can be stated as follows:

> No element is coded in such a way that its code appears, digit for digit, as the *first part* of any element code of greater length.   (12)

How does that solve the problem of telling where an element code ends? In the following way:

When the first digit of a new element code is received, the decoder compares it to his list of one-digit element codes. If he finds a matching element code on the approved list—otherwise known as the source code—he has identified the element and he knows that the next digit begins a new element. If he doesn't find a matching element code on that one-digit element code list, then he knows the element code is incomplete; he reads the next digit in the transmission, and then compares the two-digit combination with his list of two-digit element codes. Once again, if there's a match, the element code is complete. If not, it's incomplete, and the next digit must be read, to make a three-digit combination. Obviously, this end-signalling device won't work if the first three bits of a five-digit element code happen to be the same as the three bits of some three-digit code. In such a case the longer element code would be mistaken for the shorter one, and the decoder would then attempt to interpret the last two bits of the five-digit code as part of the next element code, probably making nonsense of the whole transmission.

On the other hand, if the Prefix Property is satisfied, then no shorter element code will be a prefix of any longer one, and "complete" or "incomplete" can be signalled by the presence or absence of a matching element code in the source code listing. Decoding is said to be *instantaneous* with a prefix code.

We are free to number the elements in any order that we choose, and we can therefore number them in such a way that:

$$P(1) \geq P(2) \geq \cdots \geq P(N-1) \geq P(N). \tag{13}$$

Given 13, it follows that in an optimum code we must have

$$L(1) \leq L(2) \leq \cdots \leq L(N-1) \leq L(N). \tag{14}$$

Suppose that (14) were false. Then $L(3)$ might be greater than $L(7)$, for example, and in that case, the more probable element would have the longer string of coding digits. Then we could improve the source code simply by interchanging the two element codes, and thereby shorten the average element code length. But the source code cannot be considered optimum, until no more such improvements are possible. Therefore, in an optimum source code, line 14 will be satisfied; that is, the length of a given element code will never exceed the length of a less probable element code.

Several elements may have the same probability. That's why (13) is written with greater-than-or-equal signs. In an optimum source code, can their element codes be different in length? Yes. If no way can be found to shorten the longer element codes in such a subset of equiprobable element codes, then the source code is optimum. We can interchange such codes among themselves in any way without affecting the average element code length; and in particular, we can arrange them in such a way that both (13) and (14) are satisfied; that is, we can give the longer element codes the higher numbers, to satisfy (14).

Before we get into the proofs of the three remaining restrictions, it will be useful to define *prefix* and to clarify Restriction (b):

The $k$-th prefix of an element code will be defined as the first $k$ digits of that element code. Basic restriction (b) will then be satisfied if:

> No element is coded in such a way that its code is a prefix
> of any other element code, or that any of its prefixes are used     (15)
> elsewhere as element codes.

As (14) now stands, it allows the last and second last element codes to be of different length. But in an optimum code, we will find that they are the same length.

Let us see why this is so. Suppose that they were different in length. Suppose the last is 19 digits and the second last is 17 digits. We already know that the first 17 digits in the last or $N$th element code are not the same, digit for digit, as the 17 in the second last—by the prefix property. (See (15) above.) By the same prefix property, we know that the first 17 digits of the last element code are not the same as the 17 digits of any other 17-digit element codes, if there happen to be any. There aren't any longer element codes, after the last one, of which those first 17 digits in the last element code might be the 17th prefix. And finally, by the same prefix property, no code shorter than 17 digits coincides with any of the shorter prefixes in the first 17 digits of the last element code.

Therefore, the decoder can distinguish the first 17 digits of the last element code from all the other element codes in the source code, and so there's no reason to retain all 19 digits. The last two digits are excess baggage, and we can reduce the *ACL* by cutting them off.

Therefore, in an optimum source code we will find that the two longest element codes are the same length. Changing (14) to express this fact, we obtain

$$\text{\textbf{Restriction (c):}} \quad L(1) \le L(2) \le \cdots \le L(N-1) = L(N). \tag{16}$$

We now know that at least two element codes, if not more, will be of length $L(N)$. The next point to be demonstrated is that in an optimum code, at least two of these element codes will be identical except for their final digits.

Suppose it were otherwise. That is, suppose that each of the element codes of length $L(N)$ had a different $(L(N) - 1)$st prefix. Suppose $L(N) = 17$. By the prefix property, no shorter code would be identical with any of the 16-digit prefixes in the 17-digit codes, and no shorter code would be identical with any shorter prefix (of less than 16 digits) in the 17-digit codes. The first 16 digits of the 17-digit codes would therefore be distinguishable from each other and from all shorter codes, and therefore, the 17th digit would be excess in these codes and we could reduce the *ACL* by cutting it off. But in an optimum code, there are no excess digits; and so, if the source code is optimum, at least two of the element codes of length $L(N)$ must be identical in their first $(L(N) - 1)$ digits.

> There may be more codes of length $L(N)$ beside the last and
> second last, but they cannot be identical in their first $(L(N) - 1)$
> digits to the last and second last, because their $L(N)$th digits     (17)
> would make them identical with either the last or second last,
> violating Restriction (a).

Putting together the conclusions reached in the last few paragraphs, we have another restriction on the source code:

> **Restriction (d)** In an optimum binary source code, the two
> least probable element codes (the $N$th and $(N-1)$st) will be     (18)
> identical except in the last bit.

To obtain the fifth and last restriction, let us suppose that there existed a sequence of the two coding symbols that was less than $L(N)$ digits long, but was neither an element code nor a prefix of an element code, and had none of its prefixes used as element codes. Then this sequence might be substituted for the $N$th element code, and the *ACL* thereby reduced. But if the source code is optimum, no such improvements are possible.

Therefore, in an optimum source code, any possible sequence of $(L(N)-m)$ digits $(0 < m < L(N))$ must either

—be used as an element code, or

—have a prefix that is an element code, or

—be a prefix of an element code,

and in particular:

**Restriction** (e)   With the exception of the $(L(N) - 1)$st prefixes of the codes of length $L(N)$, each possible sequence of $(L(N)-1)$ digits must either be used as an element code or must have one of its prefixes used as an element code.   (19)

The foregoing statement (e) expresses the last of Huffman's derived restrictions on the source code.

## B.  A Huffman Code Satisfies the Requirements

Huffman's method of binary code construction has already been explained in connection with the solution of Exercise 18. Essentially, one constructs a tree, whose branches divide into two and only two branches at every fork; and the branching is continued, until there is a twig for every element in the source. By labelling the two upper branches 0 and 1 at every fork, we build up a code that describes, for each element, a unique path from the trunk to the twig. It's clear enough that such a code satisfies Restrictions (a) and (b), that is, that each code be unique and that no code be a prefix of any other.

In the remainder of Part B, we show that a Huffman code will satisfy Restrictions (c), (d), and (e); and then, in Part C, we complete the proof of minimum redundancy by showing that no alternate code that satisfies the restrictions can have a shorter average code length than a Huffman code.

Restrictions (c) and (d) say that two of the least probable element codes must be (1) the same length, and (2) identical in every bit but the last, and (3) that no element code shall be exceeded in length by the code for a more probable element (as specified by the running inequalities in (13) and (16)).

Observe that if point (3) just above is taken for granted, then the least probable element codes cannot be exceeded in length by any others, and points (1) and (2) can be restated to require merely that there shall be no less than two element codes of the greatest length, and two of these shall be identical in every bit but the last.

Now, suppose that 1110111 is an element code.  Then the Huffman method of construction guarantees that 1110110 is either a code, or the seventh prefix of two or more longer codes. But if the coding tree in question has no paths longer than seven digits, then 1110110 must be a code, and behold, we find that if no codes are longer than seven digits, there must be two of that length, differing only in their final digits.

In the Huffman code construction process, we satisfy points (1) and (2) above by putting the two least probable elements (or two of the least probable, if there are more than two probabilities of the smallest or second-smallest magnitude) on two twigs of the tree that spring from the same fork, and labelling those twigs 0 and 1 respectively.  The path from the trunk to that fork is undetermined at that stage of the construction, but it will be the same for both elements and will be represented by the same string of digits, thus ensuring that the $(L(N) - 1)$st prefix is the same for both, as required.

At this point we must introduce the concept of *auxiliary sources*. When the two smallest probabilities in the original source are combined into a composite, the set of $N - 1$ probabilities made up of that composite and all the remaining elementary probabilities is called the *first auxiliary source*.

To guarantee that this new source called the *first auxiliary* is coded in the most efficient way, we must arrange for its two least probable members (be they composites or elementaries) to have element codes the same length and differing only in their final digits. We do this by joining the two least probable members of the first auxiliary source in a new composite, and applying the labels 0 and 1 to the branches of the resulting new fork. Now, one of these members may be a composite, and if so, its code is a prefix of two longer codes (those for the two smallest probabilities in the original set). Nonetheless, the procedure satisfies the requirement that the element codes for the two least probable members *of the first auxiliary source* be the same length and differ only in their "final" digits (final from the point of view of the first auxiliary source).

After the two smallest members of the first auxiliary source are combined, the remaining set of $N - 2$ composites and elementaries is known as the *second auxiliary source*, and of course, we satisfy the requirements for the codes of its two least probable members in the same way as before. Thus, the Huffman process guarantees that in each of the successive auxiliary sources, the two least probable members have codes the same length and differ, as required, only in their final digits (relative to that auxiliary).

Recall now that Restrictions (c) and (d) were spelled out into three points, of which the third was that a Huffman Code will satisfy the running inequalities of (13) and (16). Those who are not prepared to take point (3) for granted are invited to find a shorter proof than the following:

To show that Huffman's construction satisfies point (3), we need only show that

$$\text{IF} \qquad P(j) < P(i), \tag{20a}$$

$$\text{THEN} \qquad L(j) \geq L(i) \tag{20b}$$

provided only that the codes are constructed by the Huffman process, that is, by the rule that two probabilities $U$ and $V$ <u>may</u> be combined if and only if there exists no third probability $W$ that is <u>less than</u> the greater of $U$ and $V$, and that $U$ and $V$ <u>must</u> be combined if and only if there exists no $W$ that is <u>less than or equal to</u> the greater of $U$ and $V$. Must a programmer take other steps to guarantee (20a, b), or will adherence to the rule be enough?

$$\text{Let} \qquad P(j) = A < B = P(i). \tag{21}$$

We shall use $L(A)$ and $L(B)$ as shorthand notations for $L(j)$ and $L(i)$ respectively.

(I) If no unequal probabilities like those in (21) can be found in the source, then the source probabilities are all equal to each other, and (20a, b) cannot be violated.

The following definitions will be useful:

> ELIGIBLE: A probability $Q$ (elemental or composite) is <u>eligible</u> for combination if there is available no more than one other uncombined probability (elemental or composite) that is <u>less than</u> $Q$. (22)

> MANDATORY: An eligible probability $Q$ is <u>mandatory</u> for combination if there is available no more than one other eligible that is <u>less than or equal to</u> $Q$. (23)

OPTIONAL: $Q$ is optional if it is eligible but not mandatory.     (24)

These definitions are illustrated in the figures below:

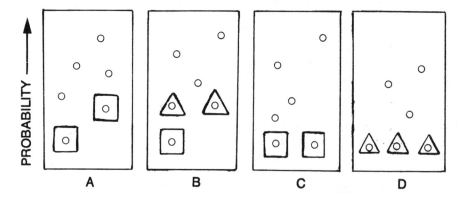

|     |     |     |     |
|:---:|:---:|:---:|:---:|
| A   | B   | C   | D   |

In Figures A, B, C, D any circle (probability value) enclosed by a square or triangle is eligible.  Those enclosed by squares are mandatory.  Those enclosed by triangles are optional.

(II) When the Huffman process arrives at a stage such that $A$ is eligible for combination, $A$ may form a composite either with $B$, or with some other value, call it $F$ ($F \leq B$).  Observe that $B$ cannot combine, except with $A$, while $A$ remains uncombined; so both these outcomes remain available, if $A$ remains uncombined until $A$ is mandatory.

(III) If $A$ and $B$ combine, then $L(A) = L(B)$ and (20a, b) are satisfied.

(IV) If $A$ combines with some other value $F$, then either

$$(A + F) < B \tag{25}$$

$$\text{or}\ \ (A + F) > B \tag{26}$$

$$\text{or}\ \ (A + F) = B \tag{27}$$

(V) If (25), then $L(A)$ has gained a digit, and $L(B)$ has no digits yet, and the process returns to step II above, $(A + F)$ and $B$ now playing the roles of $A$ and $B$.

(VI) If (26), observe that $(A+F)$ cannot then combine, except with $B$, while $B$ remains uncombined.  When $B$ becomes eligible, $B$ may combine either with $(A + F)$ or with some other value, call it $G$.

(VII) If $B$ combines with $(A + F)$ in VI above, then $L(A)$ gets a second digit at the same time that $L(B)$ gets its first digit. The further digits added to the two codes in later stages of the process are identical, and so $L(A) = L(B) + 1$, and (20a, b) are satisfied.

(VIII) In VI above, if $B$ combines with $G$, then $G \geq F$, for if $G < F$, then $A$ would have combined with $G$ rather than $F$; and so we have

$$F \leq G, \tag{28}$$

$$A < B \qquad \text{by hypothesis}, \tag{29}$$

$$(A + F) < (B + G). \tag{30}$$

In (30), the composite containing $A$ is smaller than the composite containing $B$; the codes for $A$ and $B$ have one digit each, so there's no violation of (20a, b); and the process returns to step II, with $(A+F)$ and $(B+G)$ in the roles of $A$ and $B$.

(IX) The third possibility in step IV was

$$(A+F) = B. \tag{31}$$

In such a case $B$ and $(A+F)$ will become eligible simultaneously. At that stage of the Huffman process, there either will be, or will not be, one and only one uncombined value $X$ that is less than $B$.

(X) If there is an $X < B$, then $X$ is mandatory and it may combine

$$\text{with} \quad B \tag{32}$$

$$\text{or with} \quad A+F \tag{33}$$

$$\text{or with} \quad C = B, \quad \text{if such a } C \text{ exists.} \tag{34}$$

Note that $X \geq F$, for the same reason that $G \geq F$ in step VIII.

(XI) If (32), then $A$ and $B$ are parts of composites $(A+F)$ and $(B+X)$. We know

$$F \leq X, \tag{35}$$

$$A < B, \quad \text{so} \tag{36}$$

$$(A+F) < (B+X) \tag{37}$$

and the situation is the same as (30), step VIII, with $X$ in the place of $G$.

(XII) If (33), then we have

$$(A+F)+X > B. \tag{38}$$

At this point, $B$ remains eligible; it combines either

(a) with $[(A+F)+X]$, in which case the $A$ code will be two digits longer than the $B$ code, satisfying (20a, b), or else:

(b) $(A+F)+X$ remains uncombined until $B$ combines with some other value $Y$. Now, $Y \geq B > X$ (because $X$ was the sole value remaining less than $B$). We then have

$$A+F = B \tag{39}$$

$$X < Y, \quad \text{so} \tag{40}$$

$$(A+F)+X < B+Y. \tag{41}$$

Here in line 41 the $A$ code is *one digit longer* than the $B$ code, and $A$ is in the smaller composite. The process returns to step II, with $[(A+F)+X]$ and $(B+Y)$ in the roles of $A$ and $B$ respectively.

(XIII) In step X, if (34) occurs, then $C$ takes $X$ out of the picture so far as $A$ and $B$ are concerned, and we then have a situation identical to the second alternative in step IX, that is,

$$A+F = B, \tag{42}$$

both are eligible, and there is NO uncombined $X < B$. Now, either $(A + F)$ and $B$ will combine with each other (making $L(A) = L(B) + 1$ and so satisfying (20a, b)), or else

$$B \text{ combines with } Z = B, \tag{43}$$

$$\text{or } (A + F) \text{ combines with } Z = B. \tag{44}$$

(XIV) If (43), then $(A + F) < (B + Z)$, $L(A) = L(B)$, and we are back at step II again with $(A + F)$ and $(B + Z)$ in the roles of $A$ and $B$, and $A$ in the smaller composite.

(XV) If (44), then

$$(A + F) + Z > B, \tag{45}$$

and $B$, remaining eligible, combines either

$$\text{with } \quad (A + F) + Z \tag{46}$$

$$\text{or with } H \geq Z = B, \tag{47}$$

where $H \geq Z$ because otherwise, $(A + F)$ would have combined with $H$ rather than $Z$.

(XVI) If (46), then $L(A) = L(B) + 2$, and (20a, b) prevail again.

(XVII) If (47), and $H > Z$, then

$$A + F = B, \tag{48}$$

$$Z < H, \tag{49}$$

$$(A + F) + Z < B + H, \tag{50}$$

and we return to step II again, with $A$ in the smaller composite and $L(A) = L(B) + 1$.

(XVIII) If (47), and $H = Z$, then

$$A + F = B, \tag{51}$$

$$Z = H, \tag{52}$$

$$(A + F) + Z = B + H. \tag{53}$$

From (53), we return to step IX, (31), with $(A + F)$ in the role of $A$, $Z$ in the role of $F$, and $(B + H)$ in the role of $B$; $L(A)$ and $L(B)$ have both gained a digit, but $L(A)$ remains one digit ahead, just as before. The cycle from (31) to (53) and return may repeat itself if there are more pairs of equal $Z$'s and $H$'s to fill those roles, but the cycle must end at last because the source is finite.

(XIX) In all the possible stages of the process, we see that the digits gained by the $A$ code either equal or exceed those gained by the $B$ code; we never see the $B$ code gaining more digits than the $A$. In the end, therefore, we must have $L(A) \geq L(B)$, as declared by (20).

Now, let's consider whether Restriction (e) is satisfied. Basically, that question amounts to this: can we begin at the trunk of our coding tree, and proceed upward through any number of forks to a fork one of whose branches leads neither to an element, nor to another fork? If we could find such a fork, then by coding the path from the trunk to that fork, and then to that branch, we would obtain an unassigned code, possibly shorter than $L(N)$. But there are no such forks in a Huffman coding tree.

As an exercise, check the following three-digit binary codes against a properly constructed set of Huffman codes, the longest of which exceeds three digits in length:

$$000 \quad 010 \quad 100 \quad 110$$
$$001 \quad 011 \quad 101 \quad 111$$

These are all the possible three-digit binary codes. You will find that every one of these eight codes either (1) is an element code in the Huffman set, or (2) has a prefix that is an element code, or (3) is a prefix of an element code. Thus none of them is available to improve the Huffman coding through substitution for the longest code in the Huffman set.

## C. Conclusion

The Huffman coding procedure leads to a sequence of auxiliary sources, as explained above. The first auxiliary has $N-1$ members (one composite and $N-2$ elementaries). The second auxiliary source has $N-2$ members—either 1 composite and $N-3$ elementaries, or 2 composites and $N-4$ elementaries. As each auxiliary is formed by combining two members of the previous auxiliary, it follows that each auxiliary has one less member than its predecessor, and in general, the $k$th auxiliary has $N-k$ members.

Let $WH(N)$ be the average code word length or ACL for the Huffman coding of a set of $N$ elements, and let $WA(N)$ be the ACL of an alternate coding of the same set of $N$ elements, and suppose that

$$WA(N) < WH(N). \tag{54}$$

If that's true, then the alternate is more efficient than the Huffman.

The smallest probability in the set may be unique, or there may be several having the least value; and the second smallest likewise may or may not be unique.

One of the two or more longest codes in the set of Huffman codes must represent an element $A$ whose probability $P(\min)$ exceeds no other in the set; and another code of equal length must represent an element $B$ whose probability $P(\min^1)$ exceeds no other but possibly $P(\min)$ itself. This much is guaranteed by the running inequalities of (13) and (16), which the Huffman code fulfills by (20a, b) which were proved above. Thus we have

$$p(A) = p(\min) \leq p(\min^1) = p(B) \leq p(\text{non} - A, \text{ non} - B) \tag{55}$$

Observe that $A$ and $B$ are element *names* here, and no longer stand for probability *magnitudes* as in Part B above. Their codes are identical in all bits but the last, as shown in Part B above.

In the alternate code, likewise, there must be two or more codes of the greatest length because that is a requirement for an efficient code as shown in

Part A. One of the two or more longest must represent an element C (perhaps not identical to A) having probability $p(\text{min})$; and another of equal length must represent an element D (perhaps not identical to B) having probability $p(\text{min}^1)$. These two smallest probability values $p(\text{min})$ and $p(\text{min}^1)$ must be among those represented by the longest codes, because otherwise the alternate code will not satisfy the running inequalities in (13) and (16), which were shown to be requirements in Part A. Furthermore, the alternate codes for these elements C and D must be the same length and differ only in their final digits, because those are also requirements laid down in Part A. If the alternate code doesn't meet all those requirements, it can't be better than the Huffman, which does meet them.

We must emphasize that $p(\text{min})$ has the same numerical value for both codings, because they are being applied to the same source elements; and likewise, $p(\text{min}^1)$ has the same numerical value for both codings.

Without changing $WH(N)$ or $WA(N)$, we can rearrange the element numbering in both codes, if necessary, so that the elements A and B having probabilities $p(\text{min})$ and $p(\text{min}^1)$ are the $N$th and $(N-1)$st in the Huffman coding, and the elements C and D having the same two probabilities $p(\text{min})$ and $p(\text{min}^1)$ are the $N$th and $(N-1)$st in the alternate coding.

Thus in both codes

$$p(N) = p(\text{min}), \quad \text{and} \tag{55}$$

$$p(N-1) = p(\text{min}^1). \tag{56}$$

We know that

$$WH(N) = ACL = \sum_{i=1}^{N} p(i)LH(i), \tag{57}$$

where $LH(i) = $ the length of the $i$th element code
in the Huffman coding. $\tag{58}$

Expanding (57),

$$WH(N) = LH(N)p(N) + LH(N-1)p(N-1) + \sum_{i=1}^{N-2} p(i)LH(i). \tag{59}$$

But $LH(N) = LH(N-1)$, so (59) becomes

$$WH(N) = LH(N)[p(\text{min}) + p(\text{min}^1)] + TH(N-2), \tag{60}$$

where

$$TH(N-2) = \sum_{i=1}^{N-2} p(i)LH(i). \tag{61}$$

Now let

$WH(N-k) = $ the $ACL$ of the $k$th auxiliary source
in the Huffman construction. $\tag{62}$

At this point, recall that in the first auxiliary source, all the original elements survive except the $N$th and $(N-1)$st. These two elements are combined;

## C. Conclusion

the probability of the composite element is $[p(\text{min}) + p(\text{min}^1)]$; and *in the first auxiliary source*, the code word length of the composite element is $(LH(N)-1)$. The average codeword length (*ACL*) *of the first auxiliary source* is therefore given by

$$WH(N - 1) = (LH(N) - 1)[p(\text{min}) + p(\text{min}^1)] + TH(N - 2). \tag{63}$$

By subtracting the *ACL* of the first auxiliary source (in (63)) from the *ACL* of the original source (in (60)), we obtain

$$WH(N) - WH(N - 1) = p(\text{min}) + p(\text{min}^1). \tag{64}$$

In the alternate coding, things are much the same as in the Huffman, so we find

$$WA(N) = LA(N)[p(\text{min}) + p(\text{min}^1)] + TA(N - 2). \tag{65}$$

And

$$WA(N - 1) = (LA(N) - 1)[p(\text{min}) + p(\text{min}^1)] + TA(N - 2). \tag{66}$$

Subtracting (66) from (65), we obtain

$$WA(N) - WA(N - 1) = p(\text{min}) + p(\text{min}^1). \tag{67}$$

Thus, comparing (64) and (67), we find that the *difference* in the *ACL*, between the original source and the first auxiliary source, is the same for the Huffman coding and the alternate coding; that is,

$$WH(N) - WH(N - 1) = WA(N) - WA(N - 1). \tag{68}$$

Observe that we have obtained (68) without assuming that the longest element codes in the two codings are the same length. That may or may not be true.

The next step would be to compare the differences in the *ACL*s between the first and second auxiliary sources in the Huffman and alternate constructions. Here we may find that $p(\text{min})$ and $p(\text{min}^1)$ have different values than in the first stage, but they are the same for the Huffman and alternate codings. In the alternate scheme, the coding of the first auxiliary source must meet all requirements, just as they are met in the Huffman coding of the first auxiliary source (or the alternate cannot be more efficient). And so we must find that

$$WH(N - 1) - WH(N - 2) = WA(N - 1) - WA(N - 2) \tag{69}$$

and in general, that

$$WH(N - k) - WH(N - k - 1) = WA(N - k) - WA(N - k - 1). \tag{70}$$

Now, as the *k*th auxiliary Huffman source has $N - k$ members, therefore the $(N - 2)$nd has *only two* members. These two members will be coded by the single digits 0 and 1, so obviously the *ACL* at that stage will be:

$$WH(2) = 1. \tag{71}$$

In the alternate coding, the *ACL* begins at the value *WA(N)*, and then is reduced to *WA(2)* by a sequence of decrements that are exactly equal *in magnitude and number* to the decrements that make up the whole difference between *WH(N)* and *WH(2)*.

Thus, if

$$WA(N) < WH(N), \tag{72}$$

as we supposed in (54) above, it follows that

$$WA(2) < WH(2) = 1. \tag{73}$$

But *WA(2)*, the average codeword length of a source of only two members, cannot be less than unity and therefore (72) is impossible.

We conclude that no alternate coding can give a smaller average codeword length than the Huffman coding: the requirements that were shown in Part A to be necessary are satisfied by the Huffman code as shown in Part B, and are now shown to be sufficient to guarantee a code having the least possible average code word length.

This does *not* mean that the Huffman procedure can give only one result for a given source. For example, the source 1/3, 1/3, 1/6, 1/6 can be Huffman coded in two ways, both having 2 bits as the average word length; but in one coding every word is 2 bits, while in the other, the word lengths are 1, 2, 3, and 3 bits respectively. In such a case, the coding of lesser variance is often preferred.

# Answers

## Answers to Exercises

**1.** 2 bits/measure.

**2. a.** $R_2R_3R_2R_1$

   **b.** $R_1R_1R_1R_1R_1R_1R_1R_1$

   **c.** $R_3R_2R_2R_3R_1R_1R_3R_1R_3R_1$

   **d.** $R_1R_1R_4R_4R_2R_2R_2R_3R_3R_3$

**3. a.** Your choice.

   **b.** $R_1R_2R_1R_3R_1R_4R_2$

   $R_1R_2R_1R_3R_1R_2R_2R_2$

**4.** Yes.

**5. a.** 1010000110110

   **b.** 00100110111

**6. a.** $R_2R_2R_1R_1R_1R_1R_1R_3R_4R_3R_1$

   $R_1R_1R_2$

   **b.** $R_1R_1R_2R_3R_4R_1R_1R_1R_1R_2R_3$

**7.** Your choice.

**8.** $\log_2(1/4) = -2$ since $2^{-2}$

   $= 1/4$

   $\log_2(1/2) = -1$

   $\log_2(2) = 1$ since $2^1 = 2$

   $\log_2(4) = 2$

   $\log_2(1/16) = -4$

   $\log_2(1) = 0$

   $\log_2(1/256) = -8$

   $\log_2(1/4096) = -12$

**9.** $\log_2(6/10) = -0.74$

   $\log_2(3/10) = -1.74$

   $\log_2(1/1000) = -9.97$

   $\log_2(99/100) = -0.015$

**10. a.** $I = -\frac{1}{2}\log_2\frac{1}{2} - \frac{1}{2}\log_2\frac{1}{2}$

      $= -\log_2\frac{1}{2} = 1$

   **b.** 2

   **c.** 1.75

**d.** 2.75

**11. a.** 0.881

   **b.** 0.722

**12. a.** You did this calculation before (Exercise 10d). The entropy was 2.75.

   **b.** This is the best we could do:

| | |
|---|---|
| $L_1$ | 00 |
| $L_2$ | 01 |
| $L_3$ | 100 |
| $L_4$ | 101 |
| $L_5$ | 1100 |
| $L_6$ | 1101 |
| $L_7$ | 11100 |
| $L_8$ | 11101 |

The average code word length is:

$\frac{1}{2}(2) + \frac{1}{4}(3) + \frac{1}{8}(4) + \frac{1}{8}(5)$

   $= 23/8 = 2.875$ bits/code word.

According to Shannon we should be able to do better. Read on.

**13.** Yes.

   Yes.

**14.** 1 bit/code word.

**15.** No. See the next exercise.

**16.** The entropy is approximately 0.88.

**17.** The average code word length is:

   $.49(1) + .21(2) + .21(3) + .09(3)$

      $= 1.81$ bits/digram or

      $.905$ bits/letter.

**18.** This problem is solved in the section on Huffman coding.

**19.** Entropy = 4.080

**20.** 5.

**21.** Code 2: 4.869   Code 3: 4.080

**22.** $2^8 = 256$
$2^9 = 512$

**23.** The cost in bits per letter for the code is:

.03(2)+.16(2)+.81(1) = 1.19.

The digrams, probabilities and codes are:

| | | |
|---|---|---|
| AA | .0009 | 1111111 |
| AB | .0048 | 1111110 |
| BA | .0048 | 111110 |
| AC | .0243 | 11110 |
| CA | .0243 | 11101 |
| BB | .0256 | 11100 |
| BC | .1296 | 110 |
| CB | .1296 | 10 |
| CC | .6561 | 0 |

The cost of this code is 1.7438 bits per digram or 0.87 bits per letter, a big improvement over monogram coding. The entropy for the source probabilities .03, .16, and .81 is (from Table 1):

[.03(5.0589)+.16(2.6439)
    +.81(.3040)]
    =.821 bits per letter.

**24.** The binary number equivalents for 35, 43, 65, and 97. They are:

#: 0100011
+: 0101011
A: 1000001
a: 1100001

The word SUPER ... IOUS has 34 letters. The number of bits required is 34 × 7 or 238 using either upper or lower case letters.

**25.** Answer given by computer program.

**26.** Upper case: 333 bits.
Lower case: 225 bits.

ASCII: 238 bits.

**27.** 0, 0, 1, 0, −1, −54, 255, −155, 155, −255.

**28.**

| $x$: | 0 | +10 |
|---|---|---|
| $p(x)$: | $329 \times 10^{-3}$ | $305 \times 10^{-5}$ |

Check your remaining answers against Table 5.

**29. a.** 6 bits

**b.** 3.45 bits

**c.** Regular, 3.4897; modified, 3.5001.

**d.** Approximate increase = .0396 bit = $p(3) - p(7)$.

Exact increase = .0362, allowing for shortening the 32 longest codes by 2 bits each.

**30.**

| Gray Level | Parity Bit | Extended Code |
|---|---|---|
| 2 | 1 | 00101 |
| 3 | 0 | 00110 |
| 7 | 1 | 01111 |

**31.**

| ASCII Character | ASCII Code | Parity Bit | Extended Code |
|---|---|---|---|
| # | 0100011 | 1 | 01000111 |
| + | 0101011 | 0 | 01010110 |
| A | 1000001 | 0 | 10000010 |
| a | 1100001 | 1 | 11000011 |

**32.**

| Received Code | In Error |
|---|---|
| 11000011 | No (the number of ones is even) |
| 11000110 | No (the number of ones is even) |
| 10000000 | Yes (the number of ones is odd) |

**33.** I LO_E YOU.

**34.**

| Gray Level | 3-Redundant Code |
|---|---|
| 4 | 000111000000 |
| 7 | 000111111111 |

**35. a.** 0101 or gray level 5

**b.** 0111 or gray level 7

**36. a.** 4/5 × 4/5 × 4/5 =.512

**b.** 9/10 × 9/10 × 9/10 =.729

**c.** $(19/20)^3$ =.857375

**d.** $(99/100)^3 = .970299$

**37.** Same answer as that for the complementary case of 000 being transmitted. The answer is 112/125.

**38.** If 00000 is submitted to the channel it will be correctly decoded by majority vote decoding if any of the following strings is received:

| | | |
|---|---|---|
| 00000 | 00011 | 10001 |
| 00001 | 00101 | 10010 |
| 00010 | 00110 | 10100 |
| 00100 | 01001 | 11000 |
| 01000 | 01010 | |
| 10000 | 01100 | |

The probability of receiving all 0's is $(4/5)^5 = .32768$.

The probability of receiving four 0's and one 1 is $(4/5)^4 \times 1/5 = .08192$.

The probability of receiving three 0's and two 1's is $(4/5)^3 \times (1/5)^2 = .02048$.

Hence the probability of receiving one of the strings listed is $.32768 + 5(.08192) + 10(.02048) = 0.94208$.

So the bit-error rate is $1 - 0.94208 = 0.05792$.

**39.** The array with parity check is

01001
01010
01100
01111

**40.** The first row and first column have an odd number of ones

11001
01010
01100
01111

**41.** 0111100: gray level 12.

0100101: gray level 5.

0010110: gray level 14.

The underscored bits are check bits.

**42.** The first check indicates no error in bits 1, 3, 5, 7. The second check indicates no error in bits 2, 3, 6, 7. The third check indicates an error in bits 4, 5, 6, 7. By deduction bit 4 is incorrect and the received code 1101110 is decoded as 1100110 which is gray level 6.

**43. a.** All three parity checks show no error so 0101010 is decoded as 0010 (gray level 2).

**b.** The first check indicates no error in bits 1, 3, 5, 7. The third check indicates no error in bits 4, 5, 6, 7. The second check indicates an error in bits 2, 3, 6, 7. By deduction bit 2 is incorrect. So 0001010 is decoded as 0101010 or gray level 2.

**c.** The first check indicates an error in bits 1, 3, 5, 7. The second check indicates an error in bits 2, 3, 6, 7. The third check indicates no error in bits 4, 5, 6, 7. By the first and second checks either 3 or 7 is in error. The third check shows bit 7 is correct so bit 3 is implicated as the incorrect one. So 1110110 is decoded as 1100110 or gray level 6.

**d.** The first check shows an error. The second and third checks show no error. Hence bit 1 is incorrect. So 1010110 is decoded as 0010110 or gray level 14.

**44.** Syndromes are **a.** 000 **b.** 010 **d.** 001.

**45.** $r = 4/7$.

**46.** Some students find this problem difficult.

You need 4 checks here. The bit positions checked by the parity bits are:

bit 1 checks bits 1, 3, 5, 7, 9, 11;

bit 2 checks bits 2, 3, 6, 7, 10, 11;

bit 4 checks bits 4, 5, 6, 7;

bit 8 checks bits 8, 9, 10, 11.

So, for example the exclamation point (!) whose ASCII code is 0100001 has the Hamming code 01011001001.

last check is not satisfied. Hence, a single error has occurred and it must be in the last bit. So all of the information bits are correct. These appear in positions 3, 5, 6, 7, 9, 10, 11 and are 0100001 which represents the exclamation point again.

# Answer to Questions in Appendix I

**A.1.** Referring to the answer to Exercise 46 you see that you must do the 4 original parity checks on

1. bits 1, 3, 5, 7, 9, 11;
2. bits 2, 3, 6, 7, 10, 11;
3. bits 4, 5, 6, 7;
4. bits 8, 9, 10, 11.

In addition you must do a parity check on all bits 1, 2, 3, 4, 5, 6, 7, 8, 9, 10, 11, 12.

For part a of the exercise, you discovered that all 5 parity checks are satisfied (even number of ones), indicating no errors, so the code sent, given by bit positions 3, 5, 6, 7, 9, 10, 11, is 0100001 which is the ASCII code for exclamation point.

Checking the code for part b of the exercise you find that the second check and the check on all bits are not satisfied. So you have detected two errors, but you do not know the positions of the errors. You could request a retransmittal of this codeword.

Checking the code for part c of the exercise, you discover that all 4 original checks are satisfied, but the